Scholes

MY STORY

MY STORY

Scholes

WITH IVAN PONTING

SIMON &
SCHUSTER

London · New York · Sydney · Toronto · New Delhi

A CBS COMPANY

To Claire, Arron, Alicia and Aiden

First published in Great Britain by Simon & Schuster UK Ltd, 2011
A CBS Company

1 3 5 7 9 10 8 6 4 2

Simon & Schuster UK Ltd
1st Floor
222 Gray's Inn Road
London
WC1X 8HB

www.simonandschuster.co.uk

Simon & Schuster Australia,
Sydney

Simon & Schuster India,
New Delhi

Every reasonable effort has been made to contact copyright holders of material
reproduced in this book. If any have inadvertently been overlooked, the publishers
would be glad to hear from them and make good in future editions any errors
or omissions brought to their attention.

A CIP catalogue record for this book is
available from the British Library

ISBN 978-0-85720-607-7

Printed and bound in Great Britain by
Butler Tanner and Dennis Ltd, Frome, Somerset

MIX
Paper from
responsible sources
FSC® C023561

CONTENTS

FOREWORD

BY SIR ALEX FERGUSON

Manchester United have been blessed down the decades with a galaxy of fantastic footballers, some of the finest ever to walk the earth, and although these words will embarrass a dour, uncomplicated Lancashire man who has no time at all for the frivolities of life, it cannot be doubted that Paul Scholes has earned his own honoured place among the most exalted company.

As the baseline you can take Duncan Edwards, whom Bobby Charlton tells me is the best he ever played with – and that's good enough for me. Then you move forward to the unsurpassable Bobby himself; to Denis Law, who was my own hero when I was starting out in the game; and to the irresistible genius that was George Best. More recently, my own time at Old Trafford has been graced by the likes of Bryan Robson, Eric Cantona, Roy Keane, Ryan Giggs and Cristiano Ronaldo, every one of them an all-time great lauded the world over – and unquestionably Scholesy is right up there beside them.

That's why he has attracted glowing tributes from such global luminaries as Zinedine Zidane, Patrick Vieira, Thierry Henry and Edgar Davids, all unsolicited by Paul, of course – he is one of the most genuinely modest, unassuming individuals I've ever met – but palpably sincere for all that.

The first time I laid eyes on Paul was when Brian Kidd, who was our youth development officer at the time, brought him to a first-team match along with another lad and they arrived at the door of the dressing room. Kiddo told me they'd be coming so I poked my head out but didn't notice any boys. 'Where are they?' I asked. It turned out they were there all along, but both standing behind Kiddo and so small that I couldn't see them.

When Paul started to play you could see exceptional ability, but he was so tiny! One day I turned to my assistant, Jim Ryan, and said, 'He's got no chance, he's a midget.' That's become a standing joke. These days, considering all Scholesy's achieved, Jim never lets me forget that early assessment, and I have to hold my hands up. Mind, he was only about twelve at the time and he took a wee growth spurt in his early teens. As for the other lad, I let him go and he also sprouted up after he left us – he might be a policeman now!

Paul went on to be 5ft 7in or so, which is fine for a central midfield player. Look at Xavi, Iniesta, Fabregas – they're not big guys – and when we saw Spain dancing the ball about in the World Cup, wasn't it fabulous? There's always been a tradition of terrific tiny midfielders, right back to the likes of Jimmy Mason, Billy Steel and Ian McMillan in Scotland. They called McMillan 'the wee prime minister', he was that influential.

Of course, there was no getting away from the fact that Paul was small for a centre forward, his position when he came to us, and also it was clear that he didn't have the requisite pace for that role. But it wasn't too long before we realised exactly what he was, a midfielder. His extraordinary ability to play the game was never in question. His passing was always exceptional, he could play his way around any opponents in the world and other managers knew that. Not too long ago we brought him on as a substitute against Tottenham and immediately Harry Redknapp put on Wilson Palacios to man-mark him. Naturally, that didn't stop Paul.

Some people criticised his tackling but, honestly, he was never a bad tackler. He wasn't a serial offender, never did anything criminal and never really hurt anyone. He never missed a lot of games, just one here and there, nothing to worry about over such a marathon career. I know he had this wee competitive spark about him that carried him into rash challenges occasionally, and unfortunately that earned him a reputation. Did I get worried about him sometimes? Absolutely! But funnily enough, if he picked up a booking it was usually okay because he knew the possible consequences of another yellow card.

In fact, he missed far more time through injuries than suspensions, probably the equivalent of almost two seasons when you add it all up, which puts the 670-odd games he did play for United into vivid perspective.

As a person, Scholesy has an image of being quiet and so he is, but let me tell you that doesn't mean he's dull. Anything but. For instance, he's a ruthless assessor of people. He can sense a fake in a couple of seconds, seeing through all the bull every time. He won't necessarily volunteer his opinion, but if I ask him for a judgement it's instant and, where appropriate, absolutely merciless. There's no messing about, he's a completely black-and-white man, and I really love that about him.

We've had all different types of people playing for Manchester United, and not all of them have been as level-headed as Paul. He's such a wholesome character.

You didn't have to worry about where he was going in the afternoon after training, he was off back to the hills where he lives with that family of his. Most likely he'd be spending his time battering a ball about with his son, Arron. It's a fantastic way to live and it suits him. He's got a lovely family and he cherishes it. He guards his privacy strenuously and he's not changed a bit down all the years, despite the remarkable success he's enjoyed.

There's a wicked humour about Scholesy. For instance, it was never wise to go for a pee anywhere near the side of the training pitch when he was about. I can remember Gary Neville doing just that, trotting a good forty yards away from us and facing a fence. There he was, doing his business, when suddenly – whack – Scholesy's hit him on the back of the head with a sweet right-footer. He really was that accurate. John O'Shea was another victim, and he was maybe even further away. Whenever I was on the training ground I was always wary, because Scholesy was trying to catch me for years. If the players were behind me, the question was always in my mind: 'Where are you, Scholesy?'

Then there was the fun he had with big Schmeichel. At shooting practice Schmeichel would always be right off his line, maybe seven or eight yards, to make it difficult for the boys and Scholesy used to chip him, which absolutely infuriated the big

feller. One day he had steam coming out of his ears and he told Scholesy, 'You do that one more time and I'll kill you.' On Scholesy's next turn, naturally, he chips him again, beats him all ends up. Schmeichel's away like a rocket, chasing Scholesy across the pitch, lumbering along with those giant strides while the wee man's legs are pumping so hard you could hardly see them. It was hilarious, we were all falling about. That said, it was a good job Peter didn't catch him or we'd have lost a great midfielder!

Of course, Paul isn't just a wind-up merchant, there's something of the wise old head about him now. Quite a few players took counsel from him over the years, and he was, and remains, very good with the kids. He's always got a straightforward opinion and he understands everything about being a professional footballer. Quiet ones like Scholesy have got a big advantage over more demonstrative personalities because they tend to take a step back, and so they see everything. With that quality, I see a bright future for him as a coach, and there'll always be a place for him with Manchester United. He's doing his badges and one day I think he'll be excellent; he won't be the bouncy, demanding kind like Archie Knox or Steve McClaren, more a thinking man's coach like Carlos Queiroz, maybe doing things with individual players.

Just now it seems almost surreal after all these years that I'll never be able to pick him again. When he let me know his intention of retiring in May 2011, I understood his reasons and respected them absolutely. He could have gone on another year, maybe playing twenty-five or thirty games, but his professional pride wouldn't allow him to do that. He wanted to be remembered for playing fifty games a season, not half that number. That was his own analysis and he was being true to himself, which he has always been.

Paul is one in a million, and I was left to reflect on how mightily privileged Manchester United have been that he graced our team for so long. Now I can hardly wait to see him passing on all that wisdom and know-how to a fresh generation of United youngsters on the training ground. One thing is certain – they could not wish for a more magnificent role model than Paul Scholes.

Sir Alex Ferguson
Old Trafford,
September 2011

1

A BOY AND HIS BALL

I was always football daft. When I went to junior school, I would leave home half an hour early in the mornings and spend the time before the bell went for the first lesson by kicking the ball around the schoolyard. Occasionally some mates would be involved, but often I was on my own and that didn't bother me in the slightest. I was happy as long as I had that ball.

But what really fired my imagination was the prospect of getting a game. As a little lad, I was always hanging around the edge of the action when older lads were playing, just hoping they'd invite me to join in. Once I started, and they saw I was all right, then they let me play regularly, even though I was maybe two or three years younger than them. On Sunday afternoons we'd go down to the local field and play for three or four hours, then I'd go home and annoy the neighbours by kicking the ball against their fence. Football was a way of life for me from the start.

I've worked on my ball control a little bit down the years, but I think these pictures, taken by my Uncle Patrick at home in Middleton, Manchester, when I was three or four years old, demonstrate pretty clearly that I was football mad from a very early age.

◄ By the looks of the main image, I'd discovered that it helped to keep my eye on the ball, and by the way my fists are clenched, I'm determined to make it do what I want. The shot above left suggests that I might have had some idea of goalkeeping, but then again I'm practising my heading technique above right and it might be said from the way my right foot is raised that my tackling style is beginning to emerge!

The hairdo is a bit of a revelation. It's never been that long since, and I can assure you it never will be again, although perhaps the moptop look represented the cutting edge of fashion for little 'uns in the late 1970s.

I was always very close to Uncle Patrick, my mum's brother, and spent a lot of time with him when I was a kid. He loved United, travelling all over the country to watch them in his younger days, and he used to tell me all about his trips. I'm sure he played a big part in my obsession with football, which became more intense the older I got. My sister, Joanne, was never interested but if there were other kids around then I was always up for a game. If there weren't then I was happy enough to kick a ball about on my own. I could never think of a better way to pass the time. Still can't, actually.

▲ I picked up the winning habit, and plenty of sound football sense, during my time with this schoolboy team, Boundary Park. We were based in Oldham but were nothing to do with the Latics, although I did play with them during a spell in my early teens. That's me, third from the right on the front row. Manchester United fans will probably recognise Gary Neville (third from the left at the back) and Nicky Butt (second from the left at the front).

The little lad with the ball next to me is Paul O'Keefe, the son of the former Everton player and Republic of Ireland international Eamon O'Keefe. Paul joined United at the same time as me and we were pretty similar as players. Both of us were told we were too small to be footballers, but while I was lucky enough to come through the ranks, Paul wasn't and eventually he took a job outside the game. Later, ironically, he had a growth spurt which left me far behind in terms of stature.

Boundary Park was my Saturday team when I was about thirteen, and we managed to win virtually everything that was available to us. On Sundays, I played for the St Thomas More's club – you might say I was football crazy.

> *Paul was already with Boundary Park when I joined, and he might have stood out to the trained eye for his lovely skills, but as a fifteen-year-old my first thought was that he was too small. How was he ever going to compete?*
>
> **GARY NEVILLE**

◀ There's only one lad in this Manchester United youth team line-up with his socks down around his ankles. Yup, it was me, the scruffy little kid from the Langley council estate, no tidier back in February 1992 than I am today. Actually, I don't know why somebody's not told me to pull my socks up. I wasn't trying to be a rebel, I just didn't realise the state of me until now!

It's fair to say a few of the boys have spent some serious time on their hair. For instance, Robbie Savage on the left of the front row, and David Beckham next to him,

always liked a bit of gel and always made sure they looked the part for the camera. So did Raphael Burke, standing immediately behind Sav. As you can see, my barnet didn't get *quite* the same amount of attention!

I had joined United after Brian Kidd spotted me playing for the Cardinal Langley School, from Middleton in Manchester, in a final when I was fourteen. He was there to present the trophy, and he invited a few of us for trials afterwards. I've been at Old Trafford ever since.

The full line-up here is, back row left to right, Raphael Burke, Gary Neville, Simon Davies, John O'Kane, Andy Noone, Nicky Butt, Ben Thornley. At the front are Robbie Savage, David Beckham, George Switzer, Keith Gillespie, me and Chris Casper.

> *Scholesy's never been one to worry about his image. Around this time he was starting to turn heads with his talent... if not his dress sense.*
>
> **GARY NEVILLE**

> *Paul and I have been close friends since we were thirteen, we just clicked from the start. When we got the bus to the training ground at the Cliff from central Manchester, he was always the cheeky chappie, full of mischief. We'd be on the top deck and when somebody else came up the stairs, he'd shout out something, then hide behind a seat so I was left to face the music.*
>
> *Once at the Cliff he was so naughty that some first-team players put him in the tumble-dryer! Another time they put him in a big kitbag and zipped it up. I can't recall exactly what he'd done, but I'm sure he deserved it.*
>
> **NICKY BUTT**

▲ My most memorable moment in the 1993 FA Youth Cup final against Leeds was scoring this penalty in the second leg at Elland Road, but it didn't make a lot of difference as we lost 2–1 on the night and 4–1 on aggregate, having already gone down 2–0 at Old Trafford. It was nerve-wracking as I stepped up to take the kick in front of more than 30,000 fans, easily the biggest crowd I'd experienced. I'd like to say I executed it perfectly, but to be honest it was a scruffy job, the ball squeezing just under their keeper Paul Pettinger after he had dived the right way. Leeds had a decent team, including the likes of Noel Whelan, Jamie Forrester, Kevin Sharp, Mark Tinkler and Rob Bowman, and they were a bit too strong for us. I never did earn an FA Youth Cup winner's medal, having not made the team when United beat Crystal Palace in the final the previous year.

▼ Here's me with my trendy zero cut, completely shaved round the sides, having obviously visited the barber just before the final. Unlike a lot of the lads, I never had much style on my hair. I liked it nearly all cut off – it was easier to deal with. The shirt's more stylish than me – I always liked this one with the lace-up collar, which Eric Cantona and company made so famous by wearing it while winning the first two Premier League titles and an FA Cup. It's unusual for me to be in long sleeves. I preferred the short version.

I was always small, looking younger than my real age, and I was the last one of the six lads who came through together to become first-team regulars to make my senior debut – Ryan Giggs, David Beckham, Nicky Butt, Gary and Phil Neville were the others. I just developed a little bit later than everyone else. Maybe my size helped me because some of the bigger opponents might have looked at me and thought they were going to have an easy day, then I might have surprised them with something I did. I could never out-muscle anybody so I had to play a bit of football to get away from people. That made it more of a challenge for me, and I'm sure it helped to make me into a better player.

▼ To be handed the Manchester United youth team player of the year award for 1992/93 by Sir Bobby Charlton, on the emotional Old Trafford night when the club was presented with its first League championship trophy for more than a quarter of a century, was a fabulous experience beyond my dreams.

Mind, I wasn't really dressed for it. I turned up for the evening in my leather coat and had to borrow this jacket and tie from somebody else, so if it looks like I'm wearing dodgy gear I can't take the blame! At the time I didn't even own clothes like this, but it was decided I should be made to look presentable for the cameras. In fact, I'm looking like a geeky teenager (I was seventeen) while reserve player of the year, Colin McKee, appears comparatively smooth.

◄ My expression isn't giving much away, but believe me I was truly excited to be lining up for England against France in the European Under-18 championships in the summer of 1993. I started the game up front with Jamie Forrester of Leeds, but we were replaced by Queens Park Rangers' Kevin Gallen and Robbie Fowler of Liverpool, and they scored the goals in our 2–0 win.

► Looking for a pass and contesting an aerial challenge in the European Under-18 championships final against Turkey at the City Ground, Nottingham, in July 1993. I was lucky to be playing, having been brought in for my suspended United teammate Nicky Butt, and was delighted to do my bit towards lifting the trophy with a 1–0 victory. The only goal came from a penalty converted by our skipper, Darren Caskey of Spurs. Obviously my iffy technique from the spot in the FA Youth Cup final against Leeds had not recommended me for the job.

▲ The European Under-18 champions of 1993 in exuberant mood with our trophy after beating Turkey in a very tight final. It looks like Sol Campbell is leading the community chanting, and even I am joining in! It was a very fine team to be a part of, and I have terrific memories of our time together. Back row, left to right: physiotherapist Dave Galley, Kevin Gallen, Kevin Sharp, Chris Day, Andy Marshall, Sol Campbell, Rob Bowman, Nicky Butt, coach Ted Powell. Front row: Julian Joachim, me, Noel Whelan, Jamie Forrester, Chris Casper, Darren Caskey, Robbie Fowler, Mark Tinkler, Gary Neville.

◀ England's Manchester United connection. Pleased as punch, left to right, are myself, Nicky Butt, Chris Casper and Gary Neville.

2

1994/95

A NATURAL PROCESS

I never planned my football career, it just happened. Even as a lad barely out of short trousers, I was an associated schoolboy with Manchester United and somehow it never crossed my mind that the time might come when I'd have to think of a way to make a living that didn't involve kicking a ball. I was slower to develop than some of my contemporaries, but it was good to see the likes of Nicky Butt, Gary Neville and David Beckham breaking into the first team ahead of me, and reassuring to see them there when I got my big chance, against Port Vale in the League Cup in the autumn of 1994.

Later that season, occasionally I found myself starting in the Premiership alongside stars of the calibre of Eric Cantona, Mark Hughes and Roy Keane. The season ended in anti-climax as both the League title and the FA Cup slipped away, but on a personal level I felt I was moving in the right direction.

➤ I was nineteen years old, but looking considerably younger, when I made my senior debut for Manchester United in a League Cup tie at Port Vale on 21 September 1994. Although it would be unrealistic to deny that it was a very big day for me, I can say honestly that it all seemed part of a natural process which began on the morning I joined United. It's not that I ever presumed I would make the grade, only that I just did my best in every game at every level, and let the rest take care of itself. There was a full house of some 18,000 fans at Vale

Park, which might not seem a huge crowd now but it felt massive to me at the time. My mum and dad were there to see me, so was my future wife Claire, and her parents and, yes, I was really nervous, as I always was before every game. I think that's healthy – it gives you an edge and makes you ready for the contest.

◄ I was a centre forward in those days and I couldn't have dreamed of doing much better than scoring both goals in a 2–1 victory, starting with this effort to equalise after we'd gone behind early on. I managed to rob one of their defenders and found myself through on goal, then dinked the ball over the advancing keeper. I didn't have to think about the finish, it just seemed the most natural thing in the world to lift it over his head. I suppose it was down to pure instinct.

➤ As became usual down the years, David Beckham was first on the scene for the celebration, and he was pretty quick off the mark a little later when I headed the winner, too. Becks is a good lad; we were growing up together and it was brilliant to share these moments with him. As I've said, out of the group of us who came through the youth system together, I was always a little bit behind the others, whereas Becks had been in at seventeen. It had taken me a little longer to develop, and also centre forward wasn't the easiest of positions to go for, with the likes of Mark Hughes, Eric Cantona, Brian McClair and, later, Andy Cole in the road. But you have to believe that if you're good enough, then eventually you'll squeeze in – and, luckily for me, that's what happened.

❛ *Celebrating another one of Paul's great goals . . . I always seemed to be first there to join one of my teammates as I wanted to share their joy of scoring. I'm also a Manchester United fan so I wanted to celebrate the goal like any other fan. Scholesy scored some spectacular goals for fun. As we played together for many years, we knew each other's game instinctively. It would be great when I could pick him out with a pass and he would score. It gave me just as much pleasure setting up my teammates as scoring myself.* ❜

DAVID BECKHAM

▲ Oh dear. This might be any nine-year-old playing aeroplanes in the park with his mates, but it's not – it's me celebrating a goal in my first League game for United at Ipswich in September 1994. My son Arron is only twelve now, but he looks older than this!

Actually, this was an afternoon of genuinely mixed feelings for me, and it came only three days after my debut at Port Vale. When I was brought on as a substitute for Lee Sharpe about half an hour from the end at Portman Road we were losing 2–0. By the time I rose from the bench, the manager had reshuffled the team, with Roy Keane shifted to right-back, and pretty soon the move produced dividends. First Roy set up a goal for Eric Cantona, then three minutes later he did the same for me, charging down the right touchline, then cutting the ball back for me to tap in from six yards. Naturally, I was overjoyed. There's no feeling in the game like scoring a goal at whatever level you play. To do it in my first two matches for the senior team gave me an indescribable high – hence my antics in the picture.

Alas, my high was short-lived. Having equalised with about fifteen minutes left on the clock, I thought we'd go on to take all three points, only for Steve Sedgley to pop up with a late winner for Ipswich. That took the gloss off my day and reminded me that you can take nothing for granted in football.

◥ This picture still makes me shudder, sixteen years after it was taken. In my first season on the fringe of the team, I was lucky enough to be brought on as a substitute in the FA Cup final against Everton at Wembley. With about a quarter of an hour left, we were a goal behind and I found myself with an unbelievable chance to slot the ball past Neville Southall for the equaliser.

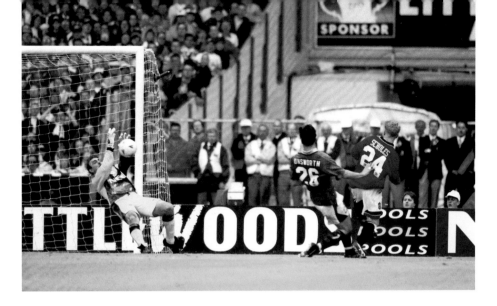

Now, I know he was a great goalkeeper, and some people say he pulled off a brilliant double save, but the truth is I made it easy for Neville to block it by hitting my first shot straight at him and then I couldn't force home the rebound. We lost 1–0 and I was devastated for weeks afterwards, thinking back to my horrible miss. Okay, it wasn't exactly an open goal, and I was under challenge from David Unsworth, but I should have done so much better. It was ages before I could bring myself to look at film of the incident. In fact, I did my best to avoid seeing it, but then I caught it somewhere by chance and felt utterly sick. Only a week earlier we had lost the League title for the want of one more goal at West Ham, and now this.

➤ This shows the full depth of my horror at what I'd just done. It looks as though I'm about to burst into tears after being foiled by Southall, and that's exactly what I felt like doing. What made it worse was that I would have to wait so long before another match in which to put the bad memory to rest.

▲ He might look like everybody's favourite uncle with a bottle and a trophy in his hands but, believe me, Eric Harrison – here being honoured for his exceptional work as Manchester United's youth coach – was one man you didn't want to upset.

He was the toughest of taskmasters and, although everybody tried to avoid getting into his bad books, we would all have received at least a couple of serious bollockings from him over the years. It wasn't something we relished at the time, but it was exactly what we needed. He gave us good habits and instilled a work ethic. Every time we trained and every time we played.

Of course, Eric wasn't just a sergeant major. He was a fantastic football man who knew the game inside and out. He taught us the Manchester United way and unquestionably he was one of the biggest influences on my career. Looking back now, I feel total respect for what he did for me, and there is affection, too. We all knew what an angry man he could be, but deep down we knew it was all for our benefit and that we owed him so, so much.

Here Eric is joined by a bevy of fresh faces who all made it to the first team. Left to right are: the old feller Giggsy looking after the rest of us, then Nicky Butt, David Beckham, Gary Neville, Phil Neville, me and Terry Cooke. I was delighted that Terry was in the picture because, just for once, I wasn't the smallest one.

3

1995/96

A DOUBLE DOSE OF GLORY

Although I managed to score fourteen goals in what might be termed my first full season of involvement in the senior side, I still didn't look on myself as a regular. But my eighteen starts and thirteen calls from the bench meant that I felt very much part of things as United lifted the League and FA Cup double for the second time in three years.

The departure of such tremendous footballers as Mark Hughes, Paul Ince and Andrei Kanchelskis during the previous summer had perplexed a lot of our supporters, particularly when there were no expensive replacements, but that did leave the field open for youngsters like myself to stake our claim for a long-term future at Old Trafford. The BBC pundit Alan Hansen wasn't convinced, making his famous observation that clubs win nothing with kids, but I think it's fair to say that on that occasion he didn't quite hit the nail on the head . . .

▲ Every striker knows that sweet split-second when you've tucked the ball past the goalkeeper and you know it's going in but it hasn't yet crossed the line. It's a fantastic feeling that I'd love to bottle, so that I could get it out and sample it whenever I fancied. This one came against Bolton at Old Trafford in September 1995 in a game we won 3–0 and in which Terry Cooke, who had been doing very well for the youth team, made a huge impact on his senior debut. Here I've just managed to reach a Ryan Giggs cross before keeper Keith Branagan and centre half Chris Fairclough, to nick the ball home in straightforward fashion. But our second goal, in which Terry demonstrated some amazing skill, was a much more spectacular affair.

He found me on the right with an extravagant back-heel, I gave him a first-time return and he crossed perfectly for Ryan to score. Afterwards one reporter compared Terry to Diego Maradona, which might have been a trifle imaginative, but I could see where he was coming from.

I grabbed my second just before the end to round off a satisfactory afternoon's work. It was my seventh game on the belt at the start of the season, easily my longest run in the team to date.

▼ For any local lad with United in his bones, this would have been a moment to savour. Just four minutes after making my first start in a Manchester derby at

Old Trafford in October 1995, I've nodded us in front against City from a Ryan Giggs corner – and to make it even more special, it turned out to be the only goal of the game. Alan Ball was the City boss at the time, and I gather he wasn't impressed that the smallest player on the pitch had been allowed to score with a header from a set piece.

Ambling up to join in the celebration, wearing that lovely infectious grin that never seemed far from his face, is Gary Pallister. He was typical of the older players in the team in making the young lads like me feel at home. You might say Pally took the mickey a little bit, but that helped us to feel part of things. He was a magnificent centre half, too, occasionally popping up to score a vital goal, so I guess Ball wouldn't have been so surprised had it been Pally finding the back of City's net.

> *Scholesy seemed a quiet one in the dressing room at first, but I soon found out he was different when he came out socialising. Paul and Nicky Butt were a great double act, giving as good as they got with the banter on a night out with the boys. Paul reminded me of Denis Irwin. He might not have been in a hurry to make his point, but when he did his humour could be quite cutting. You might call him a silent assassin.*

GARY PALLISTER

◄ What did I make of our infamous grey kit? Well, I'm not looking too happy with it here, am I? Mind you, that was nothing to do with any colour preference, more the fact that we had just lost 1–0 to Arsenal at Highbury in November 1995.

The manager made a big fuss about the strip when we were losing 3–0 at half-time at Southampton, so we changed into blue stripes for the second half. Maybe he had a genuine reason for making his point; perhaps he couldn't pick out a player against the background of the crowd and thought we might have been having the same problem. Me, I think it was more a matter of a rotten performance than dodgy kit, but all's well that ends well . . . The manager soon got rid of the grey clobber and we went on to win the League and FA Cup double that season.

◀ I hope nobody who notices my upturned collar in this picture, taken during United's home encounter with Nottingham Forest in April 1996, will imagine that I was attempting to ape the style of a certain Eric Cantona. Perhaps it was the wind, I can't remember, but certainly I would have been far too focused on the game to be bothering about how I looked.

Actually it was an afternoon on which virtually everything went right for us as we moved to the very brink of winning the title. The manager had picked me up front alongside Eric instead of Andy Cole – I'm not sure why – and shortly before half-time, just as the crowd was beginning to get a trifle tense, I was lucky enough to put us in front. And when I say lucky, I mean lucky! It looked like a decent volley into the far corner, but actually I'd shinned it and it could have gone anywhere.

Becks made it two almost immediately and then we ran in five, which was something of a marquee performance against a tough team like Forest in our penultimate game of the season. Certainly it sent out all the right signals to Newcastle, who were now the only side who could pip us to the championship.

▲ I know, I know, I don't look old enough to be drinking beer, but as I was with a couple of responsible adults there was never going to be a problem. I felt privileged beyond belief to be sat in the Middlesbrough dressing room, celebrating with the likes of Roy Keane and Steve Bruce after we had sewn up the League championship.

I was so fortunate to be playing with so many top-class footballers, who were all such terrific lads, too. Brucie would always look after you, give you bits of advice and, at the right moment, make you feel accepted by having a laugh at your expense. He could have a go at you, too, if you were in the wrong, though probably Roy was the one most likely to give you a bollocking if he thought you were stepping out of line. All the experienced players – hugely contrasting characters such as Peter Schmeichel, Paul Ince and Denis Irwin – were always on at us youngsters, spurring us on to be the best players we could possibly be. We all learned an unbelievable amount from them, and we owe them so much.

> ❛ We always wanted to make life as comfortable as we could for the young lads and banter was one sure way of doing that. Another was by using a big, industrial tumble-dryer at the Cliff, into which misbehaving youngsters had to be introduced occasionally. It might even have been switched on once or twice, but I'm not owning up to pressing the button. There are laws against that sort of thing.
>
> There was never any question about Scholesy's quality as a footballer. He was known as the little ginger magician in the youth team. Some reckon he's the best United player of the modern era, and there's a case for saying that. You don't hear him blowing his own trumpet, though – he just gets on with his job. He's the real deal. ❜
>
> **STEVE BRUCE**

◀ I might have died and gone to heaven, I was that happy when I posed in the Middlesbrough dressing room with the Premiership trophy which we had clinched with a 3–0 victory at the Riverside on the last afternoon of 1995/96. This was my first taste of being a League champion, and you might say I liked it – just a bit! Merely to play for Manchester United was amazing for me, and to actually win a major trophy so early in my career was absolutely incredible.

Once again I had started alongside Eric, but in all honesty I didn't have the greatest of games and I wasn't surprised when the manager replaced me with Andy Cole ten minutes into the second half. It proved an inspired decision because Andy scored a brilliant goal with his first touch to put us two up, following David May's early opener. Ryan Giggs added the third and, with Newcastle only drawing, we finished top of the table by four points.

▲ ▼ As a young Manchester United footballer, just how good could life get? It was a deeply meaningful question in the spring of 1996. Helping to win the club's third Premiership title in four years? Absolutely fabulous! Lifting the FA Cup, thus making up for our Wembley disappointment of a season earlier? Downright fantastic! Clinching that elusive double with a spectacular late winner from our charismatic captain, Eric Cantona, who had just bounced back from a lengthy suspension as if he'd never been away? Barely believable! Oh, and the identity of our opponents on that never-to-be-forgotten May afternoon? It was Liverpool! Come on, somebody please wake me up.

Okay, I know it was a cautious game, with the two sides cancelling each other out, and it must have bored the pants off neutrals. But for United, after all the Merseysiders' crushing dominance in the 1970s and 1980s, this was truly the stuff of fantasy. Although there was still a long way to go, at least we were on the trail towards catching up with their astonishing tally of trophies. In the game, I came on for Andy Cole after about sixty-five minutes and ran about a lot (left) but without

coming any closer to breaking the deadlock than anybody else had managed. Even such an artist as Liverpool's veteran John Barnes (far left), here shepherding the ball away from Gary Pallister and myself, could make no impact. But then came Eric's moment of divine inspiration – that perfect volley only five minutes from full time – and suddenly we were walking on air.

' *I first saw this tiny lad in the junior sides and thought he would have to punch above his weight to be a success. Scholesy did that and more. When he reached the first team it quickly became apparent that nobody would intimidate him. One day he bumped into Dennis Wise at his snarling worst at Stamford Bridge, up to all his tricks. Now Dennis is a smashing lad off the pitch, but on it he could be fearsome. That day Paul and Butty stood up for themselves, and gave plenty back with added interest. His talent was never in doubt and, after that, nor was his character or his courage.* '

GARY PALLISTER

▲ Nursing the FA Cup with Ryan, who's getting ready for a long night of celebration with an early can of beer. In fact, judging by the glassy look in his eyes, he's had at least a couple already.

The celebrations went on for two or three days, starting with a party back at the hotel with our wives, girlfriends and families. We travelled back to Manchester by train the next day with the drinks still flowing, then it was time for the traditional tour of Manchester by open-top bus – and some of us were even sober enough to make it upstairs to the top deck. Finally we dropped in at another bar for one last drink before saying goodbye for the summer. All in all, it had been a pretty decent weekend.

❝ *I always liked a celebration so probably I was just getting started. Yes, it could be my second one – I didn't realise he was counting. Was I making sure the young man didn't have an alcoholic drink? I'd have had to work very hard to do that in his case!* ❞

RYAN GIGGS

4

TRIUMPH AND TRIBULATION

Over the two campaigns of 1996/97 and 1997/98 I believe I began to mature as a player. I became increasingly integrated into the team, but was confronted with conflicting emotions as one springtime followed another.

In 1997 we retained our Premiership title, though it came as a bit of a shock when our celebrations were interrupted by the news that Eric Cantona was retiring. Then in 1998, despite enjoying an eleven-point lead over Arsenal at the end of February, we were overhauled when Arsene Wenger's team went on a fantastic late run.

The defining moment came when they beat us at Old Trafford in March with a late goal by Marc Overmars. We had a lot of players carrying knocks, but in all honesty they deserved to beat us that day and we couldn't complain when they went on to win the championship. The lack of silverware that season was dismally disappointing, but we knew we were good enough to bounce back quickly – and as it turned out, United didn't do too badly in 1998/99!

▲ We had no idea at the time, but when Ole Gunnar Solskjaer and I ran to Eric Cantona after he had scored in our crucial 3–2 victory at Blackburn on the run-in to the 1996/97 Premiership title, we were celebrating his last goal for United.

Two and a half years after making my debut I was still having to pinch myself to believe that I really was a teammate of this great footballer. At the same time he was only a man, working towards the same end as me, just doing his best like the rest of us.

Everybody is aware of the inspiration he provided on the pitch, and it's well known how dedicated he was at training, but maybe it's not so widely appreciated that he was always a brilliant bloke, too.

In those days there used to be a players' pool of cash for various commercial endorsements and when it was divided we'd all get a cheque for the same amount. On one occasion, when we were due to receive £1,500 each, it was decided that all the cheques would go into a hat, then whoever's name was drawn out would get the lot. Now £1,500 wasn't much to the older lads, but to the likes of Nicky Butt and me it was a load of cash, so really it was pretty stupid of us to be the only two youngsters to take part in the lottery. When the Frenchman won the pot, everybody was calling him 'Golden Bollocks', with Pally, Brucie and Roy being especially vocal – no surprise there! But then Eric shut everybody up by just handing the money to Nicky and me, saying that we deserved it for having the balls to take the risk. So the pair of us cleaned up and went home very happy boys, all thanks to the generous Monsieur Cantona.

▼ Was Vinnie Jones as tough as his reputation suggests? Absolutely. He really was a pretty scary character. Most people will recall how the Wimbledon players were shouting at each other, geeing themselves up to establish a psychological advantage over Liverpool as they ran out at Wembley for the 1988 FA Cup final. Well, that's how it was whenever we played them.

But you can't let yourself be intimidated or you wouldn't stand a chance of winning any game. It paid to be wary but I never allowed it to bother me. I just let it go over my head and concentrated on playing. Vinnie never said much to me anyway, and I never had any physical problems with him – maybe because he was nearing the end of his career and mellowing out a bit when I encountered him. The funny thing was, for all the stick he received for kicking people and being nasty, he could play great football as well.

In fairness, during our 1–1 draw with Wimbledon (seen in this picture here) in the FA Cup at Old Trafford in January 1997, it seems to be *me* dragging *him* to the floor, wrestling him down like a big hard man. Well, he had it coming!

◀ Who ate all the pies? Back in 1997, when these pictures were taken, obviously it was Paul Scholes. Aah, those portly days of my early twenties now seem such a long time ago. Just look at those chins – what a fine collection!

I was always prone to putting on a few pounds and back then I ate pie and chips all the time because I didn't know any different. It was just the way I had been brought up; a normal lad eating ordinary food. Going to the chippie on Thursday and Friday nights was what we did, and I had no reason to question it. I recall one youth-team trip to Switzerland with Brian Kidd and Nobby Stiles in charge when they were eating spaghetti bolognese and I didn't even know what it was. Honestly, I'd never even heard of it, and at first I wasn't impressed. It was a case of: where's my sausage and chips?

I can't deny that I was not as fit as I might have been early on. Just ask our coach, Eric Harrison. He'll tell you that I was always at the back when we went running.

I started to realise I might have to change things when we discovered that I suffered from mild asthma, the theory being that my weight might have contributed to the condition.

It was at the 1998 World Cup finals that I started losing the flab because England manager Glenn Hoddle was into the modern dietary approach. I managed to lose quite a bit then, realising that I needed to try and keep it off, and I more or less did. These days I look after myself better, which I'm sure has helped me to play for such a long time. Mind, I did a few decent things with United while I was putting away the chips, so maybe it's time for a rethink!

I like these images because they illustrate what an emotional game football will always be, with such tiny margins between success and failure, and that sometimes you can't help but let your feelings show. Clearly on the left I've just scored a goal, whereas above I've either gone quite close or goofed up altogether.

▲ He shoots, he scores! But look in the record books and you won't find this goal credited to Paul Scholes. Although we had already been crowned Premiership champions for 1996/97, we wanted to finish on a high by beating West Ham at Old Trafford in our last game of the season. After about twelve minutes I made crisp contact with a shot from just outside the penalty area and the ball shivered Ludek Miklosko's crossbar before coming down and apparently crossing the line. At least, that was my feeling at the time and afterwards it was confirmed by the camera evidence. But as the ball bounced up, Ole Gunnar Solskjaer had nipped in smartly to nod it into the net, showing exactly the type of opportunism which made him such a brilliant predator.

Now, Ole's an absolute gentleman and I'm certain he wouldn't have nicked a goal off me deliberately, but as it turned out it was a good job he reacted as sharply as he did. The referee hadn't noted it as my goal, so if Ole hadn't made sure then it wouldn't have counted.

Although the manager thought it should be given to me, Ole and I didn't even discuss it after the game. Frankly, it didn't matter who scored as long as we won, which we did 2–0, thanks to a late strike from Jordi Cruyff. I was just overjoyed to be celebrating United's fourth League title in five seasons.

▼ There is no better way to bid farewell to the fans for the summer than by showing them the Premiership trophy. This was in the spring of 1997 and for me it was the second time I was lifting that precious bauble in only two full seasons. It was a habit I hoped to get used to, the sort I never wanted to kick. I knew how lucky I was to experience this level of success playing for my local team, based only half an hour away from where I lived. There were a few years when we didn't win anything, but the ethos of Manchester United has always been to fight back – and invariably that's what we've done.

▲ ➤ It was a special joy for me to score this goal against Juventus in a Champions League group game at Old Trafford in October 1997, because they were the premier European powerhouse at that time. When the ball came through to me beyond the Juventus backline, I had a horrible suspicion I might be offside, but mercifully the flag stayed down. I found myself through on the goalkeeper, Angelo Peruzzi, who was Italy's top man in those days, and from that moment instinct took over. Certainly in these situations there is never time to ponder on whether to dribble round the keeper or attempt to dink the ball over him. This time I faked to shoot, then I managed to go round Peruzzi and pushed it into the empty net before the covering defender could get back.

Juventus were a wonderful side in the late 1990s, packed with great players such as Zinedine Zidane, Alessandro Del Piero and Didier Deschamps. We had decided the best way to approach the game was to get after 'em early, so it was a bit of a setback, to put it mildly, when Del Piero put us one down in the first minute. But Teddy Sheringham equalised, then I scored this one halfway through the second period to make it 2–1 before Ryan Giggs and Zidane both struck in the closing stages, leaving us with one of our most satisfying European victories of that era.

Unfortunately, there was an anticlimax ahead in the quarter-final against Monaco. After a goalless draw in the principality, we could manage only a 1–1 scoreline at Old Trafford and went out on away goals.

◄ Another fat day. After a lot of the goals I scored, especially in the early days, I seemed to pull stupid faces. It was almost as if I was seeing how many chins I could put on display. On the other hand, I might just have been trying to keep Gary Neville off me with his liking for, er, celebrations. That would be why the tongue's out – to keep him away! More of that later, I'm afraid.

There's no better feeling in the game than scoring a goal and this one went in at home to Barnsley in October 1997, a day we finished up with seven. It was a nice, neat one, involving a smart bit of passing with Andy Cole and Ole Gunnar Solskjaer, then a little chip over the keeper as he came out to narrow the angle.

Even so, I can't imagine what possessed me to pull quite such a daft face to the crowd. It was just a spur of the moment thing, and straight away I thought to myself, 'What on earth am I doing?' It is important, though, that the fans share our joy. Everything we do is not just for ourselves, but for them as well. They're a massive part in helping us to win games, especially the Stretford End. If we're struggling and they get behind us it really makes a massive difference.

The manager always tells us to make sure we celebrate if we score a goal, to share that precious moment of absolute satisfaction with the people who have paid good money to watch us. There's going to be enough times in any career when you suffer disappointment, so it's great to embrace the highs and transmit your emotions to the supporters. And anyway, if you've scored a goal for Manchester United, how can you not be happy?

5

TWO OUT OF THREE, CAN'T COMPLAIN

Everything came right for Manchester United in 1998/99 as we won a unique treble of Premiership title, FA Cup and Champions League. Although both Roy Keane and I were confined to seats in the Nou Camp stands for the momentous European final victory over Bayern Munich through suspension, I think I might just have accepted the overall outcome had I been offered it at the start of the season.

The manager strengthened the team significantly that season with the addition of big Jaap Stam at the heart of our defence and front man Dwight Yorke, one of the most imaginative attackers in the game. We went on a fabulous unbeaten run after Christmas and by spring 1999 the media couldn't stop talking about the treble. It was crucial that we didn't let that distract us, and we didn't. After a bit of a wobble, when we went a goal down, we took the title by beating Spurs at Old Trafford; I was lucky enough to score as we won the FA Cup against Newcastle and then I put on my club suit instead of the red shirt for the Champions League final. It wasn't how I would have chosen to spend the climax of an unforgettable campaign but, trust me, I was roaring my head off with the rest of the Manchester contingent when Ole stuck in the winner.

◄ For some unfathomable reason, posing for this ridiculous picture didn't strike me as being particularly stupid at the time, but I suppose I was young and impressionable back in 1998, whereas Ryan was old enough to have known better. He tried to wind me up, as usual, by including this shot in his own book. To make matters worse, he even came up with a load of nonsense about waiting on me in the pub, making out that it was always him who got the drinks in. It's funny, but somehow I can't remember that happening too often!

It's clear that he's entering into the spirit of the occasion — the building of a new hotel along the road from Old Trafford — rather more convincingly than me. Certainly he does look well in that hard hat, and he's got his tray perfectly poised. Not that I would ever say Giggsy's a poser, of course . . .

❛ *I think this was a case of me being told: "If you do it, then Scholesy will do it." Probably it was the only way to get him to pose for the camera.* ❜

RYAN GIGGS

➤ I'm told that Patrick Vieira has spoken very kindly of me in recent times, which is nice of him, but that's quite a contrast to at least one exchange we had on the football field during his Arsenal days. I had caught him accidentally with my elbow and he said he would f****** smash me. Fair enough, it was just heat-of-the-moment stuff and nothing ever happened. You have to accept that as part of the game and get on with it.

Vieira was a great player in his pomp, a magnificent all-rounder. He was strong, aggressive and athletic. He had tremendous skill on the ball and he had a huge physical presence. I thought he tried to bully opponents a little bit, but he could never bully United players. I've never been daunted by people being bigger than me because, after all, nearly everybody falls into that category!

I never really got to know Vieira as a person, because we never became friendly with the Arsenal team. Quite the opposite, actually. Of course, there was the famous scene in the tunnel between Vieira and Roy Keane, with Roy showing the Frenchman exactly who was the daddy, not just with words but by action on the pitch. Our skipper was a titan, as a character, a leader and as a footballer, too.

I guess you might call this a 'friendly' meeting between the two clubs, in the Charity Shield at Wembley in 1998. We lost 3–0 that day, but as we finished the season with the treble you could say that while they were victorious in this preliminary skirmish, we won the war.

▲ I've got Dwight Yorke to thank for this moment of bliss against Barcelona in the Champions League at Old Trafford in September 1998. Dwight got on the end of a David Beckham cross with a spellbinding overhead kick and when the ball bounced back off the keeper I was on the spot to bang it into the net. I was overjoyed for the team, of course, but also there was a bit of personal relief involved because I had missed a sitter against Barcelona four years earlier when I was just breaking into the side, and now I felt I was making up for my past mistake.

This goal made it 2–0 to United but unfortunately for us – although it was wonderful news for neutrals – the night's scoring was far from over. The game finished 3–3, as did the rematch in the Nou Camp a couple of months later. With the action ebbing and flowing, they were both unbelievably exciting games to play in, even if they were a bit hard on the nerves. My lasting memory of the away encounter was the mesmerising exchange of passes between Dwight and Andy Cole which resulted in Coley tucking the ball away. Absolutely sensational.

◄ This little jig of joy was prompted by the best goal I ever scored with my left foot, made all the more memorable for me because it came at the Stretford End against Liverpool, clinching a 2–0 win in September 1998.

It was towards the end of the game and we were under the cosh a little bit as Liverpool strove for an equaliser, when Andy Cole broke down the left and pulled back a low cross. Dwight Yorke reached it first, nudging it into my path and I hit the sweetest left-footer of my life from the right angle of the area. In all modesty, I have to say it gave their keeper, Brad Friedel, no chance as it flew into the far top corner. That killed off the game, which was particularly welcome as we were still smarting from a 3–0 defeat at Highbury four days earlier and needed a lift. No wonder I'm looking quite pleased.

Afterwards one of the television pundits, no doubt prompted by the Liverpool connection, called it a Kenny Dalglish-type finish, which was very flattering to me as he had been such a great player through the years when I was growing up.

▲ The determination to score against Bayern Munich in their Olympic Stadium in September 1998 is etched all over my face but, sad to say, this shot flew wide. I did manage to score that night, though, just winning a fifty-fifty race for the ball with Oliver Kahn – he might have squeaked out of the challenge a little bit – before walking it over the line. There is something deeply special about getting a goal against a really big European team, and I never tired of doing it.

► I have to pinch myself when I see a picture like this one. I'm disputing possession with Luis Figo during United's second 3–3 draw with Barcelona, this time at the Nou Camp in November 1998. As a football-mad kid, I never dreamed I'd ever be playing against global superstars like Figo; I simply couldn't conceive that it might happen to me. When it did, though, I was determined not to let the opportunity pass me by; I knew I had to concentrate like crazy to try and make my mark. Of course, when you're on the pitch, superstar reputations don't come into it. There are that many great players around you that you could easily spend all your time worrying and never get anything done yourself. But you never forget that these immense footballers can make you look silly at any moment, and that forces you to concentrate still further.

Figo cruised around the pitch, never seeming to get out of first gear, but he always appeared to have time on the ball. He could beat players in the blink of an eye, or shoot, or cross, or slip through a cute little pass to make a goal. Mind you, he was once nutmegged by John O'Shea. But then, Sheasy has nutmegged everybody in his time . . .

▲ Stretching out a leg to block a cross from Vegard Heggem as Liverpool mount a rare attack during one of the most one-sided FA Cup encounters I can remember at Old Trafford. The trouble was, after eighty-eight minutes of almost total United domination we were still behind to an early header from Michael Owen. We had rattled the woodwork a couple of times; we had seen plenty of goal-bound efforts scrambled off the line; but as time ticked away we'd have been more than happy to get a replay. Cue the most exciting and ultimately satisfying finish to any game I ever played in.

First, David Beckham's free kick was cushioned perfectly by Andy Cole for Dwight Yorke to tap in an equaliser. Then, deep into stoppage time, the ball came to me in the Liverpool box. As I tried to go round a defender it squirted away from me and I thought the chance had gone, but it ran to Ole Solskjaer who hit it through the legs of Jamie Carragher and into the net.

◀ To beat Liverpool at any time is wonderful; to do it in this manner just defied description. Devastating for them? Yup, and the more devastating the better as far as we were concerned. With our history of rivalry, we didn't care about their feelings. Just look at our celebration, above right, with Roy Keane flying over the top as usual. We're ecstatic.

Very little was said between the two sets of players afterwards, not even at international get-togethers. Even with England, we were never that friendly with the Liverpool contingent. Robbie Fowler was okay, but we never palled up as a group. I don't think they liked us really. Maybe there was a lot of jealousy because we were winning things all the time.

▼ In the autumn of 1998 as the title race began to take shape we played Leeds, always among our bitterest of rivals, at Old Trafford. Here I am congratulating Nicky Butt on a goal fit to win any match and one of which any player in the world would have been justly proud. Nicky took a pass from Phil Neville on the edge of the box, killed the ball with one sublime touch, then swivelled on the proverbial sixpence to beat England keeper Nigel Martyn with an absolute belter.

Nicky was a terrific all-round footballer, the type you would never want to play against. He was brilliant in the air, he could tackle, pass, defend, attack, you name it, and he was a hard lad who knew how to look after himself.

Scoring wasn't his main job when he got into the first team, but prior to that he'd been prolific at all levels. In fact, we used to have bets on who would score the most times in a season – and that was when I was a centre forward and he was in midfield!

United have always had so many obviously talented players that he tended to be overlooked when the praise was handed out, but within the game he was never underestimated. We all knew exactly how good Nicky was – and so did Pele, who named him the player of the 2002 World Cup.

◀ I hate missing any part of the preparation for the game, so it's no wonder I'm so miserable here, looking sombre on the sidelines at training with an icepack strapped to my knee. Some players don't seem to mind at all if they have to sit out a session. In fact, I can think of lads like Gary Pallister, Brian McClair, Andy Cole, Michael Owen, who all seemed positively relieved if they didn't have to train, although when they ran out for the game they were obviously as fit as fleas. Me, I needed to do all the work I could to be sure in my head that I was ready for the fray. So on most days I was looking forward eagerly to training, it was one of the reasons I loved my job so much.

Managers differ dramatically in the stress they place on performances on the practice pitch. When Kevin Keegan was coaching England, he was always a great believer in selecting the players who trained the best. Our manager's not like that. Of course, he likes you to train well, but being brilliant on a Thursday at Carrington certainly doesn't guarantee you'll be in the team at Old Trafford on a Saturday.

We used to have a yellow jersey for the worst trainer every week, and Pally's shambolic displays ensured that it was practically his own personal property. That said, I've had it once or twice, too. Brian Kidd and then Steve McClaren both used to have a fun session on the day before a game, which is where the yellow jersey came in. These days it's a bit more serious so it doesn't tend to happen.

❛ *I just can't understand how Scholesy got the impression that I wasn't a top trainer . . .* ❜

GARY PALLISTER

▼ That's a bib David's handing me, not the dreaded yellow top for the worst performance in training. Becks worked hard in training, especially practising his free kicks. He could put a ball wherever he wanted it, and it wasn't through luck; it was because every day he was out there half an hour after everybody else had gone in, hitting free kicks into the top corner. For all the things that people say about him, Becks loves the game and gives his best every time he plays. During his time at United, nothing was too much trouble for him, no effort too great.

We all have different lifestyles, we all do different things when we go home. But so what? The only thing that should matter to others is what we do on the pitch. If people want opinions about David, let them have them about his football. Some might forget how good he was for United, but we don't – the people who were here and who really know. He was always available to receive the ball, his crosses were sublime and his work rate, like Ryan's on the other wing, was phenomenal as he ran up and down the pitch all game.

Ryan and David offered perfect balance, an ideal contrast. David's main skills were passing and crossing, and although he could run he was never going to dribble through a defence like Ryan.

As a lad, David was really, really nice, a very friendly character liked by everybody at the club. He might have been a little bit different in some ways but that was his own business. On the pitch and around the dressing room he could not have been more professional, and on a personal level he's always been a good-mannered and caring person. Whenever we meet he'll ask about my kids and the rest of my family. Genuine – that's the word that really sums up David Beckham.

' *Paul, as always, not wanting to go in the middle of the box in training . . . but, as always, he was one of the best players in training every day. We gave him the nickname "the silent assassin" as he is a quiet person but, boy, could he make himself heard when he tackled. I'm still feeling it to this day.*

Paul was an incredible professional and so dedicated. We all had that same work ethic and that is what made that team special. It was an honour to play with him. '

DAVID BECKHAM

◄ Though I missed United's unforgettable 1999 Champions League final against Bayern Munich through suspension, I did play against the Germans in both group games and I found them to be formidable opponents. They were powerful, ultra-efficient, almost robotic, although that's not to say they didn't have outstanding individual talent.

Plenty of people have commented that I am blessed with a fair old spring for such a little feller, as demonstrated in this duel with Bayern's Thomas Strunz in the 1–1 draw at Old Trafford. It wasn't something I worked on particularly, it just came naturally to me. Maybe there's an element of surprise, with opponents looking at little me and thinking it'll be easy to beat me in the air.

Even as a tiny lad I was never afraid to head the ball, I always saw it as part of the game and just got on with it. I guess I was born with an instinct for timing my leaps, which has enabled me to score a lot of goals with my head down the years. Also I've been hugely lucky to have played for a long time with two such excellent crossers as David Beckham and Ryan Giggs, which has made my job a hell of a lot easier. Denis Irwin and Gary Neville offered a consistently high-quality delivery service, too.

It seems I was born with a knack of making contact with the ball just how I wanted to, usually with my forehead. I've scored plenty of jammy goals off my knees, shins, stomach, groin and other assorted parts of my anatomy, but I can't remember any lucky headers.

▼ A few of my important goals have been thanks to a miskick and this was one of them. The scene was the San Siro, we were a goal down against Inter Milan on the night but still 2–1 up on aggregate in a Champions League quarter-final in March 1999. We had been under heavy pressure, desperately needing a goal to lift the tension, when, with three minutes of normal time remaining, Gary Neville hit a high cross into their box. The ball seemed to take an age to come down, then Andy Cole knocked it into my path. I was unmarked, eight yards out, with only the keeper to beat and scoring should have been straightforward but somehow it wasn't. I don't know what I was trying to do. I just wanted it on target but I scuffed my shot badly, maybe even catching it with my heel. As the ball rolled towards the goal I realised that I had unwittingly wrong-footed their keeper, Gianluca Pagliuca, and it crept into the corner. That was it, game over, we were in the last four, and I was left to reflect that perhaps it was a good job I didn't make a clean connection because Pagliuca might have read my intention and saved it.

The San Siro can be a very intimidating venue with its towering stands and the red-hot passion of nearly 80,000 fans. But you have to shut that out and concentrate on your own game. After all, it's just a normal-sized pitch with eleven opponents on it. The big thing is to keep the ball and give the home crowd as little as possible to cheer about. Easier said than done sometimes, though.

▲ Deep inside the second half of our Champions League semi-final first leg against Juventus at Old Trafford in April 1999, things weren't exactly going according to plan. We had conceded a potentially crucial away goal and we weren't having the best game, thanks in no small measure to the feller on the right, Edgar Davids. The Dutch midfielder was a truly mighty opponent, one of the finest I ever played against. He was everything a footballer should be, a potent cocktail of skill and aggression, power and pace, and he was at his best that night. Here he's doing his best to keep me away from the ball while it's smuggled away by his teammate, Gianluca Pessotto.

For most of the evening we struggled as a team and I didn't have a great game personally, wasting a couple of chances that I should have put away. Happily for us, the atmosphere of the tie changed in the last minute when Giggsy smashed in an equaliser from close range. It might have looked simple, but believe me it wasn't. It could easily have bounced to safety off a defender or finished high over the bar, but Ryan kept cool and did the job properly.

► I don't think anyone would accuse me of being the theatrical type, but my arms are in the air here as I know this yellow card in the second leg against Juventus in Turin is bad news for my hopes of appearing in the Champions League final. I was already carrying a caution and the possibility of another card, with its inevitable consequence, did cross my mind before the game, but once I went on as a sub for Jesper Blomqvist with only about twenty minutes left the only thought in my head was of winning the match.

The most disappointing thing about the card was that I didn't make a really bad tackle on Didier Deschamps, but when I challenged him he gave a bit of a scream, which some foreign players are liable to do, and I firmly believe that's what got me booked. I have to admit it came as a crushing blow, but there was never going to be any Gazza-type tears from me. You can get upset and disappointed, but it's only football and you have to keep some perspective. Roy Keane was in the same boat, and we were both gutted that we would miss out on the final, but it wasn't all about us. We didn't matter because United still had plenty of good players who could go to the final and do us proud. And didn't they just?

As for Roy's performance in Italy, it was majestic and it won us the game after going two down in the opening minutes. It looked like we were dead and buried, but then the skipper popped up with a brilliant header to make it 2–1 before driving us on to win 3–2. For me, this was the supreme example of his greatness. He ran the team as if he was the manager on the pitch, handing out bollockings when necessary, but always encouraging us to do better. Roy skippered us to victory so often, hundreds of times really, but this is the example that will always be remembered.

◄ I suppose it was a flight of my imagination, but somehow it seemed a darker night than usual at Villa Park in the spring of 1999. It was the epic occasion of United's 2–1 FA Cup semi-final replay victory over Arsenal and our white shirts stood out like beacons in the inpenetrable blackness. That's how I remember it anyway – a dark night lit up by Ryan Giggs.

As soon as I hear a word about that game, all I can see is Ryan with his top off, whirling it round his head in celebration of his amazing winner. I was the closest person to him as he set off on that incredible run, dancing past not just any old defenders but the likes of Dixon, Keown and Adams, some of the best in the business – and even then he still had to beat Seaman, one of the finest keepers in the world.

When you've got ten men – Roy Keane had been sent off – you need players who can run with the ball, and Ryan was the only one in our team capable of doing that. Someone said afterwards that I should have bollocked him for not passing to me because I was in a better position, but after a goal like that I'm just glad he didn't.

As he started to rip that shirt off, it felt almost as if I might be ready to tear my own off, too, as a reflex action. What stopped me? The thought of my photo-friendly body, probably!

Of course, it has entered football folklore as Giggsy's game, and really the likes of Emmanuel Petit and myself, here scrapping for possession, were mere extras. That said, the Frenchman with the blond ponytail was a tremendous operator, graceful with a wonderful left foot and a very quiet character. But he was tough, too. In the end Petit was subbed in favour of Steve Bould as they made one last desperate effort, but after Ryan's magical intervention an Arsenal comeback would have been unthinkable, and so it proved.

▼ We beat Spurs at Old Trafford on the last day of the Premiership season in 1999 to claim the first leg of the treble, here we are with the trophy. David May (right) was always at the front when there was a celebration, he just loved it. He entered club folklore when he stood on top of the pyramid in the Nou Camp. He was just warming up here.

Our keeper Peter Schmeichel wasn't exactly backward during celebrations, either. We all enjoyed them in our different ways – you might say I'm a little bit more reserved than some! I prefer to keep right out of the way whenever possible, but I must admit it's great to see my face in there with the rest on such a momentous day.

Peter wasn't quite so chirpy when I wound him up by repeatedly chipping him during shooting practice. I was only a young lad at the time while he was the best keeper in the world so I can understand him thinking I was being cheeky. He really did go ballistic, though, and chased me across the pitch. It was a good job he couldn't catch me or my career might have been cut tragically short.

➤ Strolling around Wembley before the FA Cup final against Newcastle in 1999, I was looking pretty sharp — it's obviously not a suit I've bought myself, then! You do see some dodgy suits down the years, but I really liked this one. It's just like me — nice and plain. Navy blue, smart tie — just the job, although my flower is a bit all over the place. I expect I knocked it.

Normally, I hate wearing suits. I'm definitely a jeans and T-shirt man, but I was happy to make an exception for the FA Cup final, which was always a grand occasion for me. The only thing I loathed about reaching Wembley was the whole sorry business of recording a cup final song. Ours was called 'Lift It High' and we had to dance in the dressing room where the recording was done. The whole thing was so embarrassing, I detested it.

Walking on the Wembley pitch before kick-off was always a special time, a dream for any footballer. I grew up watching the finals on TV, and I loved to see the players on the grass in their suits. It was a really big part of the day, very symbolic, and when I experienced it myself it set my stomach churning. As a lad I always loved the TV coverage, the reports from outside the team hotel, the helicopter following the team buses to Wembley — it was a ritual to me.

I know the FA Cup doesn't have the stature it used to, but still, it's fantastic to be involved in the final. Mind, no matter how plush the new stadium is, it'll never have the atmosphere of the old one. Whether it was falling down or not, it had a magic all of its own. The history seemed to ooze out of the walls. I managed to score a few goals there, which is something that'll always stay with me.

➤ It fell to me to score the second goal in our 2–0 Wembley win over Newcastle, a victory which had looked a long way off after we lost our skipper, Roy Keane, to injury soon after kick-off. But only five minutes after Teddy Sheringham had arrived as Roy's substitute, I managed to find him with a through-ball and he put us in front. Then, early in the second half, he repaid the compliment.

Teddy could have had a shot himself but I was free and screaming at the edge of the box. Intelligent player that he was, he knew exactly where I was, how I needed the ball to be played, and where I wanted to hit it. I struck it first time with my left foot, not perfectly but well enough to keep low and beat keeper Steve Harper. I didn't aim precisely, just concentrated on a decent contact, and it put us in a very strong position.

This was definitely up there with one of the favourite moments of my career. I'd lost my first FA Cup final, then in my second against Liverpool I was only on for a short time and didn't really do much. This was the one for me. To be part of winning it this time, to have made a goal and scored a goal, was unforgettable.

▲ There was no need for words as my fellow scorer Teddy Sheringham and I beamed for the cameras, each of us clutching a winner's medal in one hand and the FA Cup in the other. It was a scorching hot afternoon, Wembley was always a tiring pitch — that was part of the tradition, too — and I was totally knackered, way too tired for conversation. I just managed to complete the lap of honour, then had to summon up reserves of stamina for the party back at the hotel — although that couldn't be too wild with the Champions League final looming on the Wednesday.

Teddy is a smashing bloke. There's a bit of Cockney flashiness about him, I suppose, but I have always got on brilliantly with him. He was a phenomenal professional, looking after himself so conscientiously that he played into his forties. He had a fantastic physique and certainly loved his six-pack — he was always breathing in when the cameras were going off!

As for his football, he was a pleasure to play with. I always seemed to work well with a man who played in behind the front striker, whether it was Teddy or Dwight or Eric. I felt from the off that there was some kind of chemistry between Teddy and me, that we each knew intuitively what service to give each other. I don't think most people appreciated how hard he worked at leading the line, linking up with teammates, making it easier for us. In the fans' eyes he took a while to settle in, and some of them got on his back, but to us he was always great to have in the team.

‘ *I loved playing with Paul. We were both setters-up, we could both score goals and we were on the same wavelength, with an almost uncanny knowledge of where each other wanted the ball played. It's not often that you come across someone who understands the way you play so completely. He's a lovely lad, too, not at all full of himself. He just did the business, then went home. He wasn't one for the high life – I only saw him drunk twice and both of those times were at Christmas! One thing, though – anyone who says he couldn't tackle has got it wrong. He could tackle all right, trust me.* 🙮

TEDDY SHERINGHAM

◀ Four happy lads and one waiting for the cameraman to go away so he can put his feet up. (That's me, obviously.) Actually I was just as delighted as Ronny Johnsen, Gary Neville, Ryan Giggs and Andy Cole at winning the cup, but I was genuinely drained by my afternoon's exertions.

Ronny was a bit of an unsung hero in that team. He had a lot of injury problems and invariably after every game, sometimes even at half-time, he would have ice strapped to various parts of his body, hence his nickname 'Icepack'. But he was a terrific player, mainly a centre back but also a tremendous man-marker in midfield if needed. Ronny was quick and strong with good feet, and all over opponents like a rash. He was a magnificent defensive partner for that monster of a man, big Jaap Stam. It made such a difference to the midfielders having such a formidable pair behind us. If the ball went over our heads, we knew there was never much to worry about. The big difference between them was that when Jaap arrived he had a huge reputation, whereas few people had heard of Ronny. They soon found out about him, though.

Gary and Ryan crop up frequently in this book, but this is a good moment to speak about Coley, yet another smashing lad. He wasn't too bothered about linking play; his one thought was to score goals, which he did in abundance. When I got the ball in midfield, my first thought would be the whereabouts of whatever combination of Coley, Dwight, Ole and Teddy happened to be playing that day. Throughout his career Coley might not have got as much credit as some other strikers, but his record is staggering. He wasn't particularly bothered about training; if we did a bit of running he'd just be jogging at the back, smiling away. But when it came to doing what he was paid to do, Andy Cole was like lightning. He was one of the best finishers I have ever seen.

▲ Having done his bit towards winning the Champions League final and completing the unique treble in Barcelona, Ryan Giggs then did his wicked best to embarrass Roy Keane and myself during the lap of honour – and he can put that down as another mission well and truly accomplished.

To be honest, I didn't really even want to go out on the pitch; I would have been happy to stay in the dressing room. You see, I hadn't played and I hadn't been part of winning the cup on the night. The lads reminded me that I'd played a part in helping United get to the final, and that's true, but to me all those games were in the past. Now it was all about what happened in the Nou Camp. And how incredible was that? As much as I wanted to feel involved, there was something not quite right about standing in the middle of the lads in my suit while they were prancing about in their kit.

I don't want to sound ungrateful, and I must stress that it was really generous of Ryan and the rest to get us out there. I'm sure he felt genuinely bad for us that we had missed the match. In the end, of course, he got his way and we lifted the giant trophy, although the mischievous grin on his face as the cameras continued to pop

does speak volumes. At least I wasn't on my own, and I'm sure that Roy was every bit as embarrassed as I was. ▲

   Of course, I was overjoyed and utterly ecstatic that Manchester United had won the Champions League. If you'd seen Roy and me in the crowd at the final whistle, just behind the dugout, we were jumping about everywhere, going ballistic. The finale was all the more unbelievable because we hadn't played brilliantly and I couldn't envisage the turnaround coming. But come it did, and nothing else mattered.

❛ Okay, there might just have been a tiny bit of mischief in dragging Scholesy and Keaney on to the pitch because we knew they'd be a bit bashful, but the main reason was that they deserved to be there. They played a major part in winning the trophy by doing so much to get us into the final and we wanted them on the pitch to celebrate with us. It was a triumph for them as much as for anybody who played on the night. ❜

RYAN GIGGS

◄ We have to play football in all elements, but I do love the rain. The pitch is slicker, the ball travels quicker, it's somehow more exciting. We're running all over the place so there is no chance of getting cold and, no, you won't ever see me in a snood – I'll leave that to the foreign players. One other thing about a wet pitch is that there are always a lot of sliding tackles flying in – now, I've always enjoyed a nice sliding tackle . . .

I'm very fond of this shirt, too. It's the one in which we won the treble in 1999 and it will always have a special place in my heart. Normally, I wore long sleeves back then, something I haven't done regularly for years because I prefer the freedom of movement you feel in short sleeves. Apparently the Manchester United legend Denis Law always went for long sleeves because he could wipe his nose in them, and I guess that does make sense.

6

THREE ON THE BELT, THEN DISAPPOINTMENT

After that momentous treble in 1998/99, the winning habit took hold and we became only the fourth team in the history of our domestic game to lift three successive League championships. Throughout that period it was a joy and a privilege for me to be performing alongside such contrasting but gloriously gifted midfield partners as Roy Keane, Ryan Giggs, David Beckham and Nicky Butt. In May 2001, as I held up the Premiership trophy for the fifth time, I was still only in my middle twenties and could scarcely believe all that had happened to me during my still relatively short tenure in the first team.

When the boss added the world-class talents of Ruud van Nistelrooy and Juan Sebastian Veron to our mix for 2001/02, and we topped the table at the end of February, an unprecedented quartet of successive titles appeared to beckon, only for us to fall away and finish third. That was a bad feeling, but with the manager having reversed his earlier decision to retire at the end of the season, we were buoyant as we contemplated the future.

▲ I don't think Dwight Yorke could look down in the dumps if he tried. He was somebody who lit up your day every time you saw him. Throughout his time at Old Trafford, Dwight made it obvious that he loved life and he showed it by perpetually wearing the biggest smile you've ever seen. He was a walking, one-man tonic no matter what the situation, and when he had a goal to celebrate — like this one, my winner at home to Marseille in the Champions League in September 1999 — he was in a class of his own.

Certainly there was every reason for glee as we had just managed to pull the game out of the fire. We'd been behind to a goal by Ibrahima Bakayoko, the former Everton player, when Andy Cole equalised about ten minutes from the end. Then Dwight nodded the ball to me and I managed to scuffle past several challenges before knocking the ball in from about twelve inches. Dwight was a superb all-round footballer, and I like to think I had a similar understanding with him to the one I had with Teddy Sheringham. He was tremendous when dropping off to link with midfield, but he was equally comfortable playing as the front man. From every angle, Dwight Yorke was a wonderful player for Manchester United.

▼ In November 1999 we travelled to Tokyo to play Palmeiras of Brazil in the Inter-Continental Cup and here I am nipping past a challenge from their midfielder Zinko. It's a strange competition. On paper, it's the world championship and you have to win the Champions League just to get in it, yet somehow it's never quite taken off. Similarly with the Super Cup, which is played in Monaco, I don't think anyone in England has ever taken it that seriously, but then you see European or South American teams celebrating extravagantly after they've won it, and it makes you wonder. I might be wrong, but maybe one day it will seem a bigger deal, and it might be good to have our name in the record books for 1999 . . . I'm not holding my breath, though.

Certainly, coming in the middle of our League season it seemed a chore to go all the way to Japan and have to get used to the time change, for something which hadn't caught the imagination of either the players or the fans. Still, the manager wanted to win it, and we did, thanks to Roy Keane popping up late to score the only goal of the game at the back post.

▼ This goal, the last in a 3–0 Champions League victory over Valencia at Old Trafford in December 1999, is an illustration of how you don't have to be a giant to score with your head, no matter how tall your marker might be. David Beckham swung in a free kick from a deep position on the right touchline, I sneaked in front of their first line of defence, the big centre back Joachim Bjorklund, and managed to glance the ball into the far corner from about twelve yards. Generally, if you can get across your opponent and the delivery is right, there is simply no way he can get it before you.

Of course, it helped that David and I understood each other's methods so well. I knew exactly how he bent the trajectory of his crosses, so I had a pretty fair idea where the ball would go and I could time my run to perfection. It's not that we spent a lot of time practising the routine – United have never been a club to dwell on set pieces – rather it's about using your instinct to read the action. It doesn't work every time but it's very satisfying when it does.

▲ It looks as though I've hit a cracker here against Coventry at Old Trafford in February 2000, but although the ball ended up in their net from all of twenty-five yards, I have to admit there was a little bit of luck involved. Somebody hoisted a high ball forward to Teddy Sheringham on the edge of their box, he nodded it out to me and I volleyed it, but not cleanly or with much power. If I'd caught it properly then Magnus Hedman in their goal might have had a chance, but my bobbling daisy-cutter completely wrong-footed him and it crept inside a post. That's the way it goes. It happens so often that a slight miskick ends up in the corner. After all, if you don't know where the ball's going, what chance has the poor old keeper got?

▲ This strike, direct from a David Beckham corner at Bradford in March 2000, is one that people never let me forget and, to be honest, I wouldn't want to because everything worked out so perfectly.

As David prepared to take the kick I was walking away, as if I was going back to the halfway line, though I glanced at him just to remind him of the possibility, knowing that he was capable of finding me. Nothing definite had been planned but at the last moment I turned back towards goal. I was completely unmarked and he delivered the ball straight to my instep.

I wasn't aiming for any particular part of the net, just concentrating on hitting the rectangle, and I caught it so sweetly. There were loads of bodies in the box, which made it difficult for the keeper, and luckily for me the ball found a gap. Afterwards

somebody said it was a cert for goal of the season, but the next day Paolo di Canio scored with a truly astonishing scissor kick and my effort was in the shade. I was robbed!

◄ I loathed this kit and it slightly ruins my pleasure at seeing this picture. It was made of really funny material with baggy sleeves. The light blue pinstripe on a navy background had absolutely nothing to do with Manchester United. It was just a fashion thing and it left me cold. I always hated it when we had to wear blue anyway, because it just doesn't seem right for us. I know United have enjoyed huge triumphs in blue shirts way before my time – like winning the FA Cup in 1948 and the European Cup twenty years later – but it still feels all wrong to me.

▲ Whacking the ball with all my might from the penalty spot to complete my first hat-trick in senior club football during our 7–1 walloping of West Ham at Old Trafford in April 2000. I wasn't the regular penalty-taker but I'd already scored two and Denis Irwin, the man who usually took care of our spot-kicks, had missed one earlier in the afternoon – mind, he did tuck away the rebound off the keeper. In the circumstances Yorkie, who would have been Denis's deputy, told me to have it, and I wasn't going to argue. I have never been great with pens but we were 4–1 up at the time so the manager wouldn't have minded – I'm sure he'd take that every week. I went for power over placement and it paid off. Why am I not confident from the spot when I can actually hit the ball very crisply most of the time? I haven't got the faintest idea. Maybe it's a psychological thing, having to perform a skill in cold blood rather than doing it instinctively in the heat of the action.

► Rio Ferdinand was playing for the Hammers that day and, don't worry, he still gets a dig or two about it! To be fair, here he's beaten me to the ball and just nicked it away. I like to remind him that it was the only thing he won all afternoon. Of course, he was only a youngster at the time and this game represented a learning curve for him. For a long time now he's been a top-class operator – I don't think there's been any better defender in England for the last ten years – and I'm glad to say that since he joined us he's been on the right end of a few scorelines like this.

' *We went 1–0 up and being a young lad, still wet behind the ears from London, I thought this ain't too bad playing at Old Trafford, we could go on and win this – but by half-time we were 4–1 down. That made me realise I had a long, long way to go before I could even think about standing beside these guys and feeling I could puff my chest out. Paul took your breath away that day. He was just fantastic. He's such a selfless footballer, and also a genuine lad with a sharp sense of humour which would amaze people who only know him from his quiet public persona. He's so dry, so witty, and if someone needs cutting down to size he can do it. He'll listen for ages, then he'll pop in with one scything comment and the whole place will crack up. He doesn't seek attention, but if he needs to chuck something in then he will.* '*

RIO FERDINAND

◄ That awful kit again – the shirt looks big enough for two people – but it doesn't prevent me from hitting the top corner of Middlesbrough's net with a pretty powerful shot at the Riverside one night in April 2000. The ball had been squared to me from the right wing and I made a perfect connection so that it bent just inside the angle of post and bar.

That made it 3–1 to us after we had gone behind early on and the goal was particularly welcome because I hadn't been having the best of games, and neither had the team. Even after that we continued to be a bit shaky, but finished up winning 4–3. We were happy with that because 'Boro was always a hard place to go, especially when Bryan Robson was the manager.

▼ Was Roy Keane offering congratulations for the shot? No, just roaring with joy. He loved his celebrations and was often the first on the scene when a goal had been scored. Ryan Giggs was the one who might come up with a remark at such a moment. Nothing too profound, though, maybe something along the lines of, 'You're the man!' What he was on about I don't know . . .

▲ I know I've got an image as a quiet lad, but I have been known to venture the occasional word to a referee! My philosophy was not to keep on at the official, but if I didn't agree with something then I'd tell him. Mind, I learned a lesson one day from Paul Durkin, who is now retired. I was having a right go at him, moaning about some decision he had given against us, but he just looked me in the eye and told me to concentrate on my own game because I wasn't doing too well myself. That shook me up because it was such a good answer.

I think I got on pretty well with most refs, they all knew what I was like and how I tackled, though sometimes it seemed a bit much when I was told to watch myself even as I was walking out before kick-off. I'm certain that the majority of them didn't want to book me, but sometimes I made it impossible for them to do anything else. I tried to be careful, but bad tackles just happen occasionally. Referees do have a supremely difficult job, not one that I'd relish. Everything is analysed these days, there are cameras everywhere, and if the refs miss something – which they're bound to do sometimes because they're only human – they get a hell of a lot of abuse. Fair play, they have the guts to stand up there and do the job. Which player doesn't make mistakes in a game? Every player does, though most of them are not as highlighted as when a referee drops a clanger.

Here, during our 1–0 win at Elland Road in Febuary 2000, I don't think I'm complaining about anything too serious – probably just asking for the final whistle . . .

➤ Even though we'd strive all season to win trophies, I always felt a bit embarrassed to actually lift them up and brandish them in front of the fans. I guess you can see that here, at Old Trafford in May 2000, when we had just received the Premiership trophy after clinching the second of three consecutive titles. It's not that I didn't enjoy the celebrations – believe me, I did, and I hated it when a year went by without experiencing one – but personally I'd rather have seen the silverware being handed over to the skipper, then been able to get up and walk away. I suppose it's because the attention is on me in that moment, and I was never too keen on the limelight. I was always ready to pass on the cup to the next player in the line as fast as I could. In fact, it wouldn't have bothered me if they had missed me out altogether.

▲◀ This is one of those sublimely satisfying moments in a footballer's life that I was talking about previously. A few minutes earlier I had put us 2–1 in front against Panathinaikos at Old Trafford in November 2000 and inside the last minute we were keeping possession, making sure of the win. We just kept switching the ball around and remaining patient until suddenly, after what I found out later was an unbroken sequence of thirty-two passes, I spotted keeper Antonis Nikopolidis off his line. Though there was a risk of losing our jealously guarded possession I couldn't resist a chip, so I got my foot under the ball, and it floated beautifully over the Greek's head to nestle in the net. It was a sweet experience, not just because I scored a goal, but because the whole team had combined to perfection.

Maybe I should show these pictures to Peter Schmeichel and explain that's why I had to chip him in training, even though it made him so mad. It's always seemed strange to me when keepers take that attitude because chipping is part of the game, so why wouldn't we want to practise it? Most of them are the same, though. For instance, it was always against the law with Ben Foster and, when I was with England, Dave Seaman hated it, too. If you tried to chip him, he'd grab the ball and boot it as far up the field as he could to register his protest. It's as though keepers see it as a personal insult.

Luckily, in more recent times, Edwin van der Sar took a more liberal approach, understanding that we needed to work on our chipping like any other skill. That said, it was virtually impossible to chip Edwin. Perhaps that's why he didn't mind!

▼ A pair of head cases? Well, that's one way of putting it, because after nearly two decades of playing football with Ryan Giggs, the link-up between us on the pitch could verge on the telepathic. Sometimes when I got the ball I didn't have to look or even think, I just knew exactly where he would be and what sort of run he was going to make. That gave us an extra split-second's jump on the opposition. A huge part of being a good team is anticipating what the other lads will do in any given situation. I have felt that connection strongly with most of our regular attackers in recent years, but none more so than Ryan, as might be expected after playing together for so long.

Here we are celebrating a goal I scored at home to Sunderland in September 2000 following a lovely flowing move involving lots of players. It's all very well doing that every day of the week in training, but when it comes off in a match the feeling of satisfaction is absolutely fabulous. From the looks on their faces, the fans quite enjoy it, too.

➤ This is a belting picture. It looks like I've got a very good technique here, just the right body shape, which is what gives you power behind a strike. The fact that I've got both feet off the ground adds a bit of style, though I'm sorry to say this shot didn't bring us a goal against Bayern Munich at Old Trafford in April 2001. And as the manager might have pointed out, it's no good to display perfect shooting technique if the ball doesn't finish up in the right place.

There are quite a few images of me airborne like this, so I suppose it must have come naturally to me, but it was nothing I ever thought about, it just happened. In fact, I wasn't usually in the air when I made contact with the ball, but I tended to take off on the follow-through. Usually you don't have to put in a massive amount of muscle to get power. Sometimes if you try for maximum velocity, your head, arms and legs are all over the place and you lose any semblance of control. Far more important is nice, smooth timing. Even here I haven't tried to burst the ball, although there are a few bits of grass flying from the impact. I must have been a groundsman's nightmare, leaving a trail of divots behind me like that.

I can only imagine that Munich keeper Oliver Kahn made a great save from this effort – it's the only rational explanation!

◀ There was a big cheesy grin on my face – just for once at a presentation – as I held aloft the Premiership trophy after the final home game of 2000/01. Disappointingly we lost 1–0 to Derby County that day, which was a bit of an anticlimax for the players and fans alike. Still, nothing was going to take the shine off lifting another championship, which represented the hard work of a whole season.

The manager, looking on proudly with his medal round his neck, appears amazingly young there, which I suppose is another way of saying he's aged in the last decade. Actually, although there's a bit more grey hair now, he looks incredibly well, considering all he's done. I think the football keeps him youthful, especially with the constant introduction to the squad of so many young players.

This was our third title on the trot, which in itself was a major milestone. We'd never managed that before, although we've since repeated the achievement, which makes us the first club to accomplish it twice in more than a century of League competition. Here's to the hat-trick of hat-tricks . . .

▶ Tangling, or actually it looks closer to tangoing, with Spurs defender Christian Ziege in one of the most spellbindingly entertaining games of football I've ever played in. Manchester United's encounters with Tottenham invariably tend to be open, attractive affairs, but this meeting at White Hart Lane in September 2001 truly stretched the bounds of credulity.

At half-time we were three down, Ziege having netted with a brilliant diving header just before the break, and we were utterly shell-shocked when we returned to the dressing room. It wasn't that we had been unlucky in any way, we had just played diabolically badly. I can't recall the manager's precise words, only that they weren't nice and certainly can't be reproduced in a book which might fall into the hands of innocent children.

Yet even at that low ebb, we remembered that we were Manchester United and knew deep down that if we could get an early goal in the second half then we might just recover to steal a point. What actually happened was pure fantasy. Andy Cole, Laurent Blanc and Ruud van Nistelrooy all scored with their heads, then Seba Veron kicked a ball with his left foot, perhaps for the first time in his life, to put us in front with a fantastic goal. Finally, David Beckham finished things off with a super strike.

It was the most astonishing comeback I'd been involved in – not that I'd made much of a personal contribution, neither scoring a goal nor setting one up – but the team effort was out of this world. Of course, it can't happen every time, but it's a glorious trait of our club that if we can score once when we're in a precarious position, then we feel we can always get out of trouble.

▲ Before I even address the context of this celebration at Highbury one rainy Sunday afternoon in November 2001, I have to ask the question – when did I get a transfer to Wolves? Honestly, I fully understand the commercial necessities of modern football, but it seems almost surreal to see myself running about in gold and black. For me, those colours have nothing to do with Manchester United, and I didn't enjoy wearing them. In fact, I've disliked most of the fancier strips which the club has adopted in recent times. Call me old-fashioned, but I'm a confirmed red-and-white man and, when we have to change, let's stick with black or white. The rest? You can keep 'em!

With that off my chest, I'll continue by admitting that, despite this early goal which put us in front against Arsenal – set up for me by Mikael Silvestre, and incidentally only my first of the season, which was disappointing – this was not United's finest hour. We were poor as a team but looked like sneaking away with a draw thanks to a man-of-the-match display from Fabien Barthez, until our French keeper made a couple of mistakes near the end. Both of them were punished by Thierry Henry, so we lost 3–1.

◀ I thought I'd better include at least one picture of an enthusiastic Scholes tackle or I might be accused of evading the issue, not that there is anything horrific about this challenge on Fulham's Luis Boa Morte at Craven Cottage in December 2001. Clumsy might be the right word.

In truth, that was invariably the way of it when I landed in trouble. I don't believe I ever hurt anyone seriously with a tackle. Certainly that was never the intention. I always tried to win the ball fairly, and often I did just that. Obviously, on the odd occasion it didn't go perfectly and that could look bad.

It was very disappointing when I made one awkward tackle and got booked for it, as happened so frequently. I think that it had to be a matter of reputation. As the years went by, it felt as if some referees were less and less tolerant towards me, opting for an early booking rather than giving me a couple of chances. Yet I've seen other players commit four, five or six fouls and still not get booked. Javier Mascherano was a perfect example of that during his time at Liverpool.

If I did get carded early in a game I had to be conscious of it. There often could be a fifty-fifty ball that I thought I had a good chance of getting, but I also knew that if I didn't get there then I was almost certainly off. Of course, it had to be a snap decision and I didn't always get it right.

Despite my reputation with certain officials and with opposing fans who liked to have a laugh about it, I'm certain I didn't have a name in the game as someone who went out to hurt my fellow professionals. They knew I never went in for two-footed tackles, or intentionally went over the top. I never attempted to injure an opponent, and that's the honest truth.

◄ Laurent Blanc, here flanked by Giggsy and myself after his Champions League goal against Boavista in Oporto in March 2002, is one of the most impressive characters I have met during my time in the game, a fabulous footballer and a really nice bloke. Although he was near the end of his career when he arrived at Old Trafford, and he did love his French cigarettes, he was still in fantastic nick.

A big defender with silky skills, a typically cultured Continental performer of the sort we've never really been used to in this country, Laurent was never the quickest, even when he was in his prime and piling up the medals, but his sheer ability always got him out of trouble. I recall one astonishing drag-back in his own six-yard box against Charlton that would have been the envy of any ball artist I've ever seen, and in training he was brilliant, nutmegging people all day.

He was great in the air, too, and was very strong, well able to mix it physically when the need arose but never losing his cool. It was wonderful to play alongside Laurent, and to learn from such a top man who has everything it takes to do well in management. He made a marvellous start with Bordeaux, winning the French League, and I'm certain that he'll be a success with France. Some people reckon that one day Laurent might even take over at Manchester United, and it wouldn't surprise me. I believe he has the stature to do that and it might be a perfect fit.

► During one of those typically sunny Saturday morning showdowns at Elland Road in the early part of the last decade, here I am attempting to dart between the Leeds pair David Batty (left) and Jonathan Woodgate, both England teammates of mine and extremely decent lads.

It was always a tough fixture because the Yorkshiremen were among our keenest competitors for the title in those days, but if we were ever in the slightest doubt about the nature of the rivalry between the clubs, it would be dispelled as soon as we arrived on the team bus. Invariably we were greeted by a mob of unbelievably hostile people, positively dripping with venom and spite. I don't think there's any group of fans in the world who hated us as much as they did, not even in Liverpool. Fathers would be screaming obscene abuse at us and urging their kids to follow suit. As a family man myself, I could never get my head around that. I tried to put myself in their shoes and to think what we had done to spawn such vitriol, but even taking into account their loss of Eric Cantona to Manchester United, I couldn't come up with any sort of answer. I can only say it's deeply unhealthy and point out that, while our supporters obviously don't like Leeds, there is nothing like the same poisonous passion coming from our side of the Pennines.

Happily, these extreme feelings were never replicated on the pitch. The games were hard, and mostly extremely tight, but were usually played in good spirit. Certainly Batty was an uncompromising opponent, but he also was a tremendous player and a smashing character. He's a bit older than me and I'll always be grateful for the way he was so generous to me when I first joined the England set-up, helping me adjust to that level, even talking me through games. It was much appreciated.

This game, in March 2002, was a real thriller with United taking the points but only just, after Leeds fought back from 4–1 to 4–3, setting up an uncomfortably tense finish.

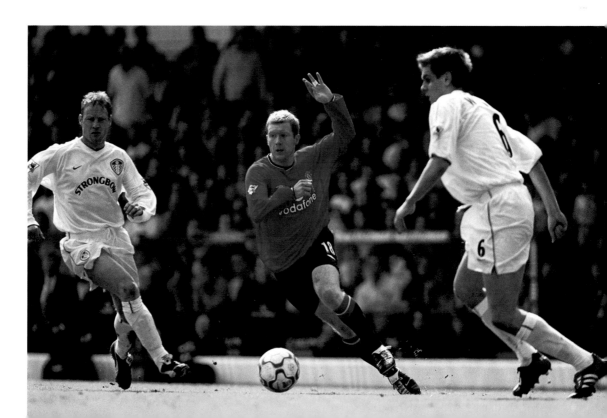

▲ The last training session before a big European game tends to have a lighter side to help the players relax, and clearly the strategy has worked here for myself, Seba Veron, Denis Irwin, Nicky Butt and Roy Keane. The picture was taken ahead of the second leg of our Champions League semi-final against Bayer Leverkusen at the Bay Arena in April 2002. Why the hilarity? Probably Yorkie had just nutmegged the manager before disappearing over the horizon.

I grew up watching Denis play for Oldham and he was always one of my heroes. He was a great defender and a terrific athlete who was superb at going forward. He was an expert with penalties and free kicks and he could cross the ball beautifully with either foot. The manager called him Mr Consistency or Mr Eight-out-of-ten and that summed him up perfectly. I remember when he came back to Old Trafford playing for Wolves; he wasn't too far off forty but he never gave Ronaldo a kick. Okay, it was one of Cristiano's first games for United, but Denis had him in his pocket.

Back in 1990 I watched Denis in action for Oldham in the two FA Cup semi-final games against United. I was already associated with United as a schoolboy but at heart I was a fan of the Latics and I took up my position at Maine Road, where the semi-final was staged, in the Oldham end with my mates. Joe Royle had put together a smashing team and they gave United an almighty fright in the first game, which finished 3–3, but they couldn't reproduce that form in the second, which they lost 4–1. Denis was brilliant in both matches, and it didn't surprise me when Alex Ferguson bought him soon afterwards.

Later it was marvellous to be playing alongside someone I had admired for so long, and also to discover that he was such a lovely bloke.

◄ Sadly, we weren't at our best in Leverkusen. In fact, we were awful on the night and I thought I was particularly terrible. In the end we drew 1–1 in Germany and went out on away goals, a hugely frustrating way to lose a Champions League semi-final, especially as we had been the favourites and our fans had been relishing the prospect of a Hampden Park final. To be honest, it surprised us how good they were, and they simply outplayed us. It was a missed chance, and so was this, a header in front of Diegio Placente which came to nothing.

▼ This is my usual position when United defend corner kicks, taking a nice little breather as I hang on to the upright. Mind, it's all very well to have a quick rest but you do have to make sure you're ready when the ball comes across. Once, when playing for England, I wasn't quite on my toes and the ball flew over keeper David Seaman straight into the top corner of the net, just where I was standing. I felt daft, and that's putting it mildly. Sometimes, of course, there's little you can do, but at least you can jump and make an effort. But on this occasion, for some unknown reason, I was transfixed and could only watch like a lemon. Clearly, guarding the posts is a crucial task at corner kicks, yet some teams don't place a man on each upright, which is curious when you think how many headers just creep into the corner.

7

NO SINGING – BUT PLENTY OF PRIDE

I didn't expect to be called up by England in the spring of 1997, even though I was happy enough with my form for Manchester United and we had just won our second successive League championship. I was twenty-two, which meant the Under-21 route into international football had passed me by, but it wasn't something I agonised over, or even thought about at all. If it happened, it happened, and if it didn't . . . well, I was more than content with the way things were going at club level.

Still, when I was picked and I got over my initial amazement at the selection, I was extremely proud. I recognised the honour and the responsibility that had been extended to me by England manager Glenn Hoddle, and I was determined to do my very best for my country, starting with my first outing, as a substitute against South Africa at Old Trafford. Is there a better place to start?

◄ I can't sing a note, so maybe it was just as well I didn't join David Beckham and manager Glenn Hoddle in a rendition of the national anthem before my England debut against South Africa at Old Trafford in May 1997. I was a bit nervous, thinking about the game ahead and wondering whether I might get called off the bench, and the thought of singing never even entered my head.

The fact that I very rarely got involved in the anthem – no more than once or twice in my sixty-six appearances for my country – certainly doesn't mean I'm anti-monarchy or anything like that. It's just that I'm usually concentrating hard on the job at hand. Neither Glenn Hoddle nor Sven-Goran Eriksson were bothered whether we sang or not, although Kevin Keegan liked the players to have a go.

Here it looks like I might be chewing gum while the others are warbling away – maybe I was lucky not to be thrown in the Tower for that!

► When I booked a holiday in New York with my girlfriend Claire – now my wife – for a few days shortly after the end of the 1996/97 season, I hadn't heard even a whisper that I might be called up by England for the coming South Africa game. But near the end of May, instead of taking in the sights of the Big Apple, here I am running around in the Old Trafford sunshine after being summoned from the bench.

My selection came as a massive surprise to me. It all happened so quickly, but I was incredibly proud to play for my country, especially to make my debut in such familiar surroundings and alongside United teammates Phil Neville, David Beckham and Teddy Sheringham, who I replaced on the pitch with about twenty-five minutes to go. England won 2–1 and I managed to nod the ball on for Ian Wright to score the winner, which wasn't the worst way to start my international career.

As for Claire, she might have been a little bit upset about missing New York, but she has always understood that there are certain sacrifices you have to make as a professional footballer. Mind, I must admit to feeling slightly bad that fourteen years have gone by and I *still* haven't taken her to the Big Apple . . .

➤ Having been caught on the hop by my England selection, I might have been excused for pinching myself to see if I was really awake when I found myself training with the likes of manager Glenn Hoddle, Paul Ince and Ian Wright. But there was no question of being overawed by the England set-up because everyone was extremely friendly and welcoming, and it helped no end to have plenty of my United teammates in the squad.

Incey was a great leader who was always talking to me when we were playing, which was ideal for a young lad like me. He and Wrighty were the best of mates, always together, always having a laugh, always accessible, making me feel part of things off the pitch and leading by their example on it.

Glenn wanted total control. He was definitely not one of the lads, and I don't think managers should be. I was grateful to him for picking me out of the blue, especially as England squads were smaller in those days so it was harder to get in. I liked him, he was a brilliant coach and he always wanted his teams to play the right way. Often he joined in with our training, and it was obvious what a fabulous footballer he had been. Certainly he had no trouble showing us everything he wanted us to do and demonstrating the standards he expected. I know he had some different ideas, such as using his alternative therapist Eileen Drewery, and to be perfectly honest that wasn't for me. But he was only trying out something new, and I don't think he should be vilified for that.

Paul Scholes was the jewel in the crown, the first name on the teamsheet and unquestionably one of the finest England players of the age. He flourished at once in the international arena, which didn't surprise me given his fabulous all-round attributes. He had almost everything – talent, intelligence, courage. His only blemish, which he never really shook off, was his tackling. There was always the chance of that red mist coming down. Overall, though, Paul was a wonderful player and he's a lovely lad, a credit to his club and to himself.

GLENN HODDLE

▲ This is my first goal for England, which came in my first start, in June 1997 against Italy in Le Tournoi, a warm-up tournament for the following year's World Cup. I really enjoyed myself that day in Nantes because we won 2–0; I managed to pass Ian Wright in for the first goal, then knocked in the second myself. I was very comfortable playing with the Arsenal striker because I felt I knew exactly what he wanted. He thrived on passes over the top of the defence, and on this occasion I managed to curl a long ball into his path from inside our own half, which was very satisfying.

My goal came at the end of a decent team move, which climaxed with Ian crossing from the left, just perfectly for me to arrive at the ball ahead of their fullback Antonio Benarrivo and knock it past the keeper, Angelo Peruzzi, with my left foot.

Before we set off for France the former United manager, Wilf McGuinness, had told me to play for my country in exactly the same way that I played for my club. This was great advice and I always did my best to follow it.

> It's important for more mature football men to speak to youngsters to help them feel good before a big occasion. I believe in giving them self-belief.
>
> Off the field, Paul appears quite shy, but on it he's like a conductor, the leader of his orchestra. He lets his passing do the talking and he's a dream to watch. 🙿

WILF McGUINNESS

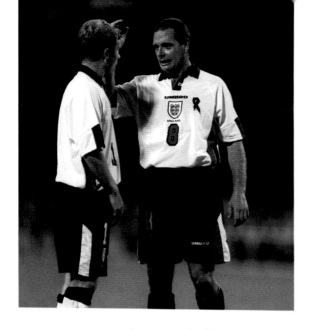

◄ It was weird to find myself in the same squad as a genius, Gazza, who was one of my heroes when I was growing up and an iconic figure all over the world. Here we are in conversation during our 4–0 win over Moldova in a World Cup qualifier at Wembley in September 1997 in which we both scored. The very thought of meeting him was a bit scary to a shy lad like me, but my philosophy has always been to try and treat star teammates like anybody else, and he was so warm and approachable that I felt at home with him from the moment I was introduced.

Gazza was brilliant to be around, one of the most generous people you could ever imagine, kind and warm but unpredictable, too. He was funny, off the wall, often saying and doing crazy things. Certainly, I've never met anybody like him, and don't expect to again. To be able to train and play with him was definitely one of the highlights of my career.

There were games in which you wanted to get the ball to him all the time because he would make something happen every time he touched it. That sense communicated itself to the rest of us and the crowd, so he lifted everyone around him. Occasionally he would do something that just defied belief, like going past five players without breaking sweat. I just wish I could have played with him when we were both at our peak; maybe we might have achieved some kind of partnership.

What's Gazza saying here? Probably telling me that he's being marked by some big fellers, so it would be better to keep the ball on the ground rather than chipping it up to him. And in case you're wondering about the black ribbon on the England shirt, it was in memory of Princess Di, who had just died.

Scholesy is one of my favourite players of all time. He was a great professional who had everything and I used to love playing with him. You could give him the ball in any position, he would take one touch and you would know exactly what the next move would be. He's a lovely bloke, too, someone who'll have a laugh but who takes his football deadly seriously. I've got loads of time for Scholesy. He was magical, pure class.

PAUL GASCOIGNE

◄ My dream start to international football continued with this goal in my first game in a World Cup final tournament, against Tunisia at the Stade Velodrome in Marseille one roasting hot afternoon in June 1998. It was near the end of the game and we were one up through Alan Shearer when the ball came to me on the edge of the box. Often you just try and whack it as hard as you can in the general direction of the posts, but this time I did try to curl it into the far corner with my right foot and for once it went exactly where I intended it to go. It was a relief as much as a pleasure because I had missed a much easier chance earlier in the game.

As a kid I never thought it was remotely possible that I'd find myself performing in a World Cup. In fact, if anybody had made the prediction I'd have told them they were stupid.

◄ You can tell the strength of the Marseille sun by the sharpness of my shadow, but in this moment of pure joy after scoring against Tunisia I must have forgotten the heat. In reality, I didn't relish the conditions one little bit. It felt like 100 degrees out on the pitch and I'm a very pale person who is simply not cut out for playing in that sort of temperature.

Although I never enjoyed being away from home for very long, this was one time when I was better off being out of the country because there followed several days of absolute madness back in Manchester. The newspapers were buzzing around my old school, interviewing my teachers, unearthing pictures of my childhood and looking for the most insignificant snippets of information about me and my life. I didn't really like it, it felt like an intrusion, but I just had to accept that it went with the new territory I was inhabiting. The fact is that if you score a goal for England in the World Cup then people want to know about you. Luckily, I wasn't at home in the middle of it all, so I was able to get down to preparation for the next game.

◄ This is one of those totally daft pictures which the press like to set up and which I hate. When you're young you just do them; when you're older you just say no. This was after the Tunisia game and I was asked to nurse the globe while pointing out the location of Romania, our next opponents. I mean, come on!

Joining the England squad had led to a profound change for me. Up to that point I'd managed to avoid performing stupid stunts for the photographers, but you have to do press conferences with England and the thought of giving interviews for the first time in my life had been a big worry to me.

As for the game, we lost 2–1. They were a good team and they outplayed us. Glenn Hoddle had been worried about Romania beforehand and now we knew why. I think the first match had taken a lot out of us physically and we were nowhere near our best for the second one.

▼ In our next game against Argentina, eighteen-year-old Michael Owen announced himself on the world stage with one of the best goals I've ever seen, and luckily I didn't spoil it for him. We were drawing 1–1 in St Etienne in the first knockout stage of the 1998 World Cup when Michael seemed to flow past half their team before finding the top corner with a perfect shot from just inside the box. I was at his elbow, and I might even have shouted for the ball, but he either ignored me or didn't see me, which was just as well given that a little later I missed a similar chance to put us 3–1 in front. If only . . .

▲ In aerial battle for England with my future Manchester United teammate, Juan Sebastian Veron, in our unforgettable World Cup clash with Argentina at St Etienne in 1998. Seba was a truly great player who was a joy to watch, and they had a few more in that category, too, with the likes of Ariel Ortega and Gabriel Batistuta.

For all that, and despite their fantastic World Cup tradition, I feel we should have won the game after playing some decent football. But it finished 2–2 and then, of course, we were beaten in the penalty shoot-out. Afterwards it was utterly devastating to watch the Argentinians celebrating, dancing on their team bus and waving their shirts around their heads. But I just had to tell myself that I'd come a long way in a short time, having been playing at international level for only a year, and at twenty-three there was still plenty of time for me. We'd gone pretty close but, if I'm painfully honest, even if we'd beaten Argentina I'm not sure we'd have been good enough to win it, given that France and Brazil were still involved.

◄ My hat-trick in a European Championship qualifier against Poland on a brightly sunlit Saturday afternoon at Wembley in March 1999 was arguably the peak of my international career. It was Kevin Keegan's first game as England boss and his reign could hardly have got off to a better start as I managed to put us into an early lead. Alan Shearer touched the ball to me in the box, I was unmarked and through on the keeper, Adam Matysek, and I was able to dink it over him as he dived at my feet. I was playing in central midfield that day, behind Shearer and my clubmate Andy Cole, and the manager had told me to get forward as much as possible. I was delighted to oblige.

▶ My second goal was a bit of a funny one. Becks put in a typically beautiful cross from the right but I couldn't quite adjust my body to meet it cleanly, and I'm still not absolutely certain how it went into the net. I believe the main impact was from my chest, but there might have been a slight contact with my arm, too. Certainly the Poland players seemed sure there was at least an element of handball, but honestly I didn't know because I was under close challenge from their defender Tomasz Lapinski when the ball came in. Even the television reruns couldn't really settle the issue, and nor does this picture. But all that mattered was that the referee was happy and we were two goals to the good after about twenty minutes of an important game.

▲ I have to admit there's a cheeky look on my face as I celebrate my second goal which might suggest I felt I'd got away with something. But, honestly, I have no clear recollection of that. I think I was just deliriously happy and very proud to have scored a goal for my country.

▲ My hat-trick goal came midway through the second half and at a crucial time: Poland, having pulled back to 2–1 before the interval, were pressing for an equaliser. Gary Neville took a long throw on the right, Alan Shearer flicked on at the near post and the ball came to me perfectly as I was running in about eight yards from the line. I had the impetus to get plenty of power behind my header and it flew past Matysek. That was the end of the scoring on a day I shall never forget.

▼ To see your name up in lights for scoring a goal at Wembley produces an incredible high, and I was lucky enough to experience it three times in one afternoon. You might say I went home happy!

➤ When Kevin Keegan greeted me after the game he seemed as happy as if he'd scored the hat-trick himself. I liked Kevin, he was someone we all wanted to do well for, a fantastically enthusiastic character who always had a good story to tell from his own playing days and who was always overwhelmingly positive. He was so passionate, a terrific motivator who loved his football and loved his country. Kevin never struck me as a man who worried about deep tactical plans. For instance, his advice to me

was to get forward as much as possible and throw a few hand grenades! Now he was bubbling with the fact that I'd managed to lob three for him against Poland.

In some quarters, Kevin was labelled as impractical because his attitude was so simple – just go out and score more goals than the opposition. Maybe he wasn't that interested in defending – certainly he seemed to leave that side of the game to his assistants, Derek Fazackerley and Arthur Cox – but he was such a great attacker as a player that it's hardly surprising he carried that attitude into his coaching work. I loved his approach, which fitted in exactly with the way I like to play, and I enjoyed his time in charge of England.

> *After my first game for Liverpool, Bill Shankly told me to go where I wanted on the pitch, to throw some hand grenades. What he meant was to cause problems for the opposition and make something happen, let people know I'd been there. I thought Paul was a similar case. I know he played deeper than I did, but he was the same type of player, a free spirit, and I wanted to give him his head.*
>
> *He had a great football brain and a superb work ethic, so I knew he'd still be doing his tracking back and I didn't want to restrict him. He was so inventive, and he had an eye for a goal, which was priceless. I'd give him ten out of ten for everything except his tackling, and nobody is brilliant at everything. And as a person I'd give him eleven out of ten, because he's a special lad.*

KEVIN KEEGAN

◄ I'm off to the Wembley dressing room to put the Poland match ball in my kitbag, accompanied by Jamie Redknapp and Philip Neville. I played quite often with Jamie, who had been in the England set-up for some time before me and had struck me as a decent, friendly lad – just the type to make you feel welcome in unfamiliar surroundings.

Of course, I was already very close to Phil, who was, and remains, one of my best friends in football after the pair of us grew up together at United. We spend a lot of time with him and his family, going out for meals, meeting at kids' parties and so on, and I'm godfather to his daughter Isabella. Since he went to Everton we're on the phone to each other two or three times a week and nothing has changed in our relationship. There was no reason why we couldn't play for different clubs but still be friends.

I was disappointed when he left Old Trafford but I could understand his need for regular football. Phil's done brilliantly well at Goodison, where he's now the captain, and I never had any doubt that he would because he's such a dedicated professional. When I first played against him it seemed odd for both of us, but we soon got over that. Now it's just a normal situation – I try to kick him and he tries to kick me!

❛ *I'm two years younger than Paul, but particularly after we both got into the England team, we spent a lot of time together. We are both family people and there was an instant rapport there. Also, he makes me laugh as soon as he opens his mouth. All the lads could be chatting and he'd be quiet, then suddenly he'd pipe up with one line that kills everybody.*

Of course, he was an unbelievable footballer, one of the best midfielders I've ever seen, and so humble with it. I don't think he knew how good he was himself. He just went to work, did his job and went home, all the while so modest in assessing himself. After I left United, sometimes I'd watch a match and then tell him he'd played like a genius; that he'd given a clinic on how the game should be played. He'd say he'd just played an average game, he never wanted any fuss. But, believe me, when he crossed that white line he was the man. He has one of the best football brains ever; he's a student of the game and he knows it inside out. When I want to talk football, I ring up Scholesy and I'm never disappointed. ❜

PHIL NEVILLE

▼ What happened to me in my next game for England after scoring the hat-trick against Poland offered a graphic illustration of the ups and downs of football life. During our next European Championship qualifier, a drab goalless draw against Sweden, I became the first England player to be sent off at Wembley. In fact, because the famous old stadium has since been demolished, I'll go down in history as the *only* England man to be dismissed on that sacred turf.

I picked up yellow cards for two rash tackles and I had no complaints; it wasn't the best afternoon I've ever had, although that was no consolation as I trudged off. I can't think of a worse place than the old Wembley to get your marching orders because there was a three-mile walk to the dressing rooms – or that's what it felt like. I felt horrible, like I'd let my teammates and my manager down. It really wasn't nice.

Typically, though, Kevin Keegan was great about it. He just put his arm around me, told me not to worry and said that these things happen. Of course, he was sent off at Wembley when he was playing for Liverpool against Leeds in the Charity Shield, when Billy Bremner also took the long walk. Probably he could have had a bit of extra sympathy for me because of that. Certainly he would have understood the sick-to-the-stomach feeling that engulfed me the moment the referee raised that second card. 'From hero to zero' doesn't begin to do it justice.

▲ Scoring the two goals at Hampden Park in the first leg of our showdown with Scotland to decide which of us would reach the European Championship finals ranks as one of my top achievements in an England shirt. The hype building up to the game in November 1999 was manic, even by modern tabloid standards, and the atmosphere on the day was fabulous.

This opener came after about twenty minutes when Sol Campbell played the ball in. I managed to nip in front of their defenders to take the ball on my chest, and then I put it away wide of keeper Neil Sullivan as he charged out to cut down the angle. Behind me, horrified but not close enough to intervene, is a young Barry Ferguson.

➤ My header which clinched our 2–0 victory came just before half-time from one of David Beckham's perfectly curled free kicks. All our big lads are in the box getting close attention – Sol Campbell, Alan Shearer, Tony Adams and Martin Keown – and obviously the Scottish defenders didn't expect somebody my size to get on the end of Becks' cross because nobody was marking me. I had all the time in the world to concentrate on hitting the target, and in it went. I was playing with a broken right wrist – the strapping is just visible – but I had a happy landing from the header and there was no further damage.

Afterwards we received an unbelievable mountain of praise in the papers, but then four days later at Wembley we were terrible, losing to a Don Hutchison goal and only just hanging on to win 2–1 on aggregate. Still, it had been an amazing experience to play in two England v Scotland encounters. In the old days when the countries met it was like a cup final, and I think the fixture should still be played now. I know there are security issues, but I believe it's wrong to strike such a massively important occasion out of the sporting calendar because there might be crowd trouble, and I feel a way should be found to police it. Dropping England v Scotland is as bad as taking away the Grand National.

▲ We'd been preparing to meet Portugal in the opening game of the European Championship for such a long time – then, suddenly, only three minutes into the action at Eindhoven, over comes one of David Beckham's flighted masterpieces from the right and I've nodded it against the bar and over the line. Abel Xavier, he of the curly blond mop who played for both Liverpool and Everton, hasn't challenged me because he was too busy looking after Michael Owen.

It was a cracking start and things got even better a quarter of an hour later when Steve McManaman doubled our lead from yet another Becks delivery. But the Portuguese were a top team and they were level by half-time, then scored the winner in the second half. We were devastated to capitulate after being in such a strong position, but in all honesty, we weren't a great side and didn't play very well at all.

◀ This shot of me at the end of the game against Portugal pretty well sums up the communal feeling in the England camp. Losing a two-goal lead is a supremely demoralising experience for any team, but we had to put it behind us and move on. One strange thing: when I'm making the header I'm wearing a short-sleeved shirt, but here I'm in long sleeves . . . I don't even recall making the change.

➤ In view of our shocking display against Portugal, I don't know why I'm looking so perky ahead of our next game, in which we faced the Germans in Charleroi. Normally I'm quite serious and concentrated before kick-off, but here I'm very relaxed. Maybe I'm tickled because Becks has forgotten to gel his hair – no, that's impossible!

Certainly, I was smiling at the end, because we beat Germany 1–0 – thanks to an Alan Shearer goal – to retain an interest in the tournament. One thing I can't help but notice here is that I'm starting to look a bit older, with some lines creeping in around my eyes and mouth. I wouldn't mind, but I was only twenty-five at the time . . .

▼ A 3–2 defeat by Romania in Charleroi ended our interest in the European Championship rather earlier than had been envisaged. Disappointment is written all over the faces of Phil Neville and myself as we arrive back at Heathrow on 21 June.

The misery was heightened for poor Phil because he was getting endless hysterical abuse in the media and from fans for making a bad tackle which gave away the decisive late penalty in our 3–2 defeat. We had only been a minute from qualifying for the quarter-finals – a draw would have been enough – so everyone felt pretty sick, but none of the players were blaming Phil. We all supported each other – that's what being in a team is all about – but in any case it would have been ridiculous to blame one poor challenge when the truth was that we just weren't good enough.

As to the flak, Phil, like his brother Gary, has had to take loads of mindless criticism throughout his career and it's a credit to both of them that they have never let it affect them. They're both strong characters and usually the stick has been so stupid that they've just laughed it off.

◄ One of the best pieces of news I received during my England career was when Brian Kidd became part of the coaching set-up. Kiddo could always make me smile – which is exactly what he's doing here during our build-up to a World Cup qualifier in Finland only three days after Kevin Keegan's shock resignation as manager – but he was also brilliant at every aspect of his job. His training and coaching routines were spot-on and he was perfect as a bridge between the players and the boss. Nobody was more effective than Brian at fostering team spirit or breaking the ice in an awkward situation, as I had found out during his time at Manchester United, where I had worked with him since the age of about thirteen. He's a very funny man, always taking the mick out of somebody in his dry way, and it was marvellous to link up with him again at international level.

Kiddo's a Manchester lad himself. During his time at Old Trafford he was tremendous with everybody, but he was particularly great with locals like me. Some coaches would speak up for the London brigade, the ones who had travelled a long way to be with United, and we always felt they were treated a little better than us. They were the ones who got any posh kit that happened to be going, while it seemed like we got nothing. But all along Kiddo felt he had a special group of home-grown footballers and, I'm happy to say, he wasn't wrong. He looked after us superbly, and we've all got a lot to thank him for.

❝ *I first saw Paul in a five-a-side schoolboy tournament in a sports hall at Middleton before I was working with United. He was very small but a lot of people were talking about his fantastic talent. Later, when Sir Alex asked me to look after the local youth scene, Paul became a priority and I found out he was at the Oldham Athletic Centre of Excellence. I wasn't going to do anything underhand, so I spoke to his parents and him about looking at United. I could understand that he was loyal to Oldham, who had a vibrant youth policy, and I never railroaded the family, I just showed them our development programme. Eventually, he did choose United, and that was fantastic news for the club.* ❞

BRIAN KIDD

▼ This was one of my better looking goals for England, a shot from about twenty yards in a friendly against Mexico at Derby in May 2001. It was a lovely summer's night, the pitch was beautiful and it was a decent game of football, which we won 4–0. It wasn't a massively important occasion, but it left me with happy memories.

▲ There was nothing spectacular about this goal, but it was an extremely important one against Greece in Athens in a World Cup qualifier in June 2001. The ball broke to me from Emile Heskey and I was able to stretch out my right leg and poke it past their keeper Antonios Nikopolidis from the edge of the six-yard box. That put us in front after about an hour of a closely fought contest but we didn't really secure the points until David Beckham scored near the end.

The Olympic Stadium is a tough place to go and it was really jumping that night. The fans were so passionate; they had plenty of richly talented players to cheer and the Greek clubs had proved they were no pushovers in European competition. So the local team's expectations were understandably high, and although they didn't qualify for the 2002 World Cup, they more than made up for that two years later when Greece became European champions.

▼ Eleven men on the threshold of a result which beggared belief: England's 5–1 victory over Germany at the Olympic Stadium, Munich, in a World Cup qualifier on the first day of September 2001. It was a mind-boggling game to be a part of and it will always be recalled by English players and fans alike with a mixture of euphoria and astonishment.

Ahead of the match, we might have been thinking that a draw wouldn't be a bad outcome, but what followed was the stuff of pure fantasy, especially after they took an early lead. It was a great all-round performance on one of those rare and happy days when everything an English player hit seemed to go in.

Michael Owen scored a sublime hat-trick and there were also goals for Steven Gerrard and Emile Heskey. The defence put in a fabulous display, too. England against Germany is the international equivalent of United taking on Liverpool and carries with it the same sort of emotional involvement. Admittedly, it wasn't the strongest German team of all time, but there was no way we were going to let that cloud our enjoyment.

Back row, left to right: Sol Campbell, Emile Heskey, Rio Ferdinand, David Seaman and Michael Owen. Front row, left to right: Nicky Barmby, Steven Gerrard, me, Gary Neville, skipper David Beckham and Ashley Cole.

◄ It will always go down as David Beckham's match, the one in which England secured the point we needed to clinch automatic qualification for the 2002 World Cup finals with a 2–2 draw against Greece at Old Trafford. The skipper played magnificently, even by his own exalted standards, capping it all with his sensational free kick which earned us the necessary result at the very death.

But as much as the game will be remembered glowingly for Becks' inspirational performance, my personal recollection of that autumn afternoon offers a vivid contrast. I had an absolute nightmare. I couldn't pass the ball to a teammate to save my life, my tackles were mistimed and I couldn't get a shot on target. Even though here it looks like I've reached the ball ahead of outfielder Kostas Konstantinidis, I'm sure I've miscued it wildly. I could only put it down as an appalling day at the office, and I couldn't wait to get home.

➤ My expression of wide-eyed innocence speaks volumes as Gabriel Batistuta appears to stumble on his way past me during England's tight encounter with Argentina at the Sapporo Dome in Japan in the group stage of the 2002 World Cup finals. Clearly there was no contact, and we went on to win 1–0, courtesy of a powerfully struck David Beckham penalty.

▼ Raindrops kept falling on my head, but this was no ordinary summer shower in Niigata, Japan, where England beat Denmark 3–0 in the last sixteen of the 2002 World Cup, after coming through group games against Sweden, Argentina and Nigeria. The downpour was so torrential that I had to wring the water out of my shirt, though I must admit it wasn't too unpleasant – at least it cooled me down. Certainly playing on a soggy evening was infinitely preferable to taking the field on a searingly hot afternoon, which we had to do in the next round against Brazil.

There's no point in dressing up the truth. When England faced Brazil in the quarter-finals of the World Cup on an unbearably hot afternoon in Shizuoka, Japan, in June 2002, we came up short. I didn't have one of my best days and too many of us didn't do ourselves justice. Michael Owen gave us a goal start midway through the first half, but after that it was all downhill for England and we lost 2–1.

Maybe we shouldn't beat ourselves up too much because sometimes you have to take your hat off to the people you're playing against. Ronaldo (above left), Rivaldo (above) and Ronaldinho (opposite) are proper players, top men who have won cups and done great things for their country. Rivaldo scored an unbelievable goal to put them level, and although Ronaldinho's winner had some luck attached to it, the simple fact is that we were not up to their quality. It's not what I would have chosen for my World Cup swansong, but that's life.

My wife and children had flown out for the game because, having got to the last eight, there was a chance that we might go all the way. The kids, Arron and Alicia, were very young, only two and one, and I don't think they were ever awake in Japan, so they were at the game without knowing it.

I have to confess I didn't enjoy the tournament, which personified all I don't like about international football – too much travelling, staying in a hotel an hour from the airport, flying here, there and everywhere for each game. Having such young children, being away from home for six weeks was no good for me. Some lads can cope, but it's something I always struggled to deal with.

▼ The England party which had gone to Japan for the World Cup were invited to a reception at Buckingham Palace in November 2002. I hope I looked respectable, if not totally relaxed, as I met the Queen. Obviously somebody had made sure my tie was straight and I don't think I let the side down when it was my turn to say hello. We didn't exactly have a long conversation and she didn't ask me about United's likely targets in the next transfer window, but it was a memorable experience to be in her company. The lad next to me is Dutch masseur Richard Smith, who looks like he found Her Majesty's joke funnier than I did.

8

BACK AT THE
PINNACLE

Success always tastes sweeter after overcoming a setback. That was exactly how it felt as the United fans rattled the Goodison Park rafters throughout our last match of the season, a 2–1 victory over Everton, with what might just qualify as my favourite tune, an appealing little ditty entitled 'We've Got Our Trophy Back'. You might deduce that my appreciation of music is, shall we say, rudimentary, and you'd be absolutely correct, but I won't lose any sleep over that. Suffice to say, the refrain remained in my head for a long time afterwards and even today it's a pleasure to hear it.

On a personal level, 2002/03 was the most successful season of my career in terms of goals scored: twenty of them in all competitions, though there was a tinge of sadness that spring with the first departure of one of the so-called 'Class of '92', when David Beckham left to join Real Madrid.

▲ I was brought up being told that the good players are the ones who always seem to have time on the ball. That stuck with me and I've always tried to find a bit of room. Without blowing my own trumpet, I think I did have an instinct for it. There's no doubt football's easier when you're in space, especially for someone like me, who was not a dribbler and couldn't go past opponents like Ryan Giggs, for example. He can be surrounded by four players and it's no problem to him. Me, I couldn't extract myself easily from that sort of situation, but if I found some space then I hoped I could put the ball where people wanted it. I suppose there must be some kind of knack to that. I don't know if it was taught to me or was something that came naturally. More likely, it was within me, just something I was lucky enough to be born with.

This is a clever shot by John Peters, the photographer who has been taking pictures of United for as long as I can remember. He has created an illusion here, as if I'm in oceans of space. I could be at Carrington; I could be in the local park; I could almost be on the moon! In fact, this was taken in the hurly-burly of a Premiership game against Fulham at Old Trafford in March 2003.

I look relaxed, in my element, 'in the zone' as they say nowadays. It's great to feel that way, to be in that moment where everything feels right, floating around the pitch without a care in the world. As I was getting older, sometimes it felt like football was hard work. Then I tried to think back to the games when it felt like I was invincible, capable of doing absolutely anything on the pitch. Those were the days.

▼ It's not like me to dribble . . . Very rarely did I try and beat people on a run because I'd much rather attempt to pass my way around them. But if somebody dived in on me and gave me the chance to nip past, like this lad from Olympiakos in Athens in October 2002, then fine, I'd have a go.

Greece was not my favourite place to play football. It's great for a holiday, I'm sure, and Athens is a stunning city, but we didn't see anything beyond airport, plane, coach, hotel and training pitch. There's a four-hour flight, then an hour and a half on a coach, and we ended up getting home at perhaps four or five in the morning, totally knackered and probably contemplating a tough Premiership game a couple of days later. I'm certainly not complaining about a footballer's lot, but it's not always as glamorous as many people might imagine.

▼ I didn't score too many goals against Arsenal, our biggest rivals for most of my career with United, so when I did hit the target, it felt very sweet. This one arrived about twenty minutes from the end of our Premiership meeting at Old Trafford in December 2002, and it wrapped up our 2–0 victory. I'd just gone past Martin Keown but he managed to get back at me and lunged in for a second challenge. He couldn't stop me from hitting the ball, though, and it took a slight deflection off him on its way into the net past keeper Stuart Taylor.

Keown was a hard and extremely effective defender, but the image many people retain of him is an unfortunate one, screaming abuse at Ruud van Nistelrooy after our centre forward had missed a penalty against Arsenal in the same fixture the previous season. In fact, Keown was a fascinating character. On the pitch he was an absolute knob as far as his opponents were concerned, but off it he was a very funny man – and that's funny ha-ha, not funny peculiar. Well, maybe funny ha-ha in a slightly peculiar way; perhaps eccentric is the word.

This was the game in which Phil Neville was sensational in midfield, standing in for Roy Keane and not giving Patrick Vieira a kick. Possibly, that's the performance which Phil is best remembered for by United fans, but I maintain his best position was fullback. He could play virtually anywhere and he always called himself 'the fireman' because he went all over the pitch putting out fires. Certainly he epitomised his nickname that day.

▲ This image is from the same game, but shows a slightly less glowing moment on my part. Having just hurdled a challenge, Thierry Henry is skipping away into the middle distance and I wouldn't have put too much money on me catching him. The only way I could have stopped him at this point would have been by tripping him, and even then I'd probably have been too late.

The Frenchman was a thorn in our side for many years, although I don't think he was ever particularly influential when visiting Old Trafford. I know he scored their goal when we beat them 6–1 – couldn't resist mentioning that! – but nothing else stands out. That said, on his day – and he had a few of them against us down at Highbury – he was absolutely scintillating, a supreme athlete and a magnificent footballer. What amazed me was that he never seemed to get a sweat on. He could run 100 metres past five or six players and he wouldn't even be breathing heavily.

I never knew him well as a bloke, although when I spent an afternoon with him promoting a computer game he came across as a really nice man. Nearly everybody who has struck me as a pain in the bum on the field turns out to be a nice guy away from the game. There must be a lesson in there somewhere.

▲ There is no more certain way of striking a stunning psychological blow against title rivals than by scoring at the death to win a game that had seemed lost, and that's what I've done here against Sunderland at Old Trafford on New Year's Day 2003.

The visitors were 1–0 up for most of the game, but with ten minutes left David Beckham ran through to equalise. After that we laid siege to the Sunderland goal, but it looked like we'd have to settle for a point until Mikael Silvestre hooked a stoppage-time cross towards me. Their keeper Jurgen Macho, who had played a blinder, came flying out and it was obvious he was going to punch the ball or punch my head. I got there just in time to nod it past him and got my nut out of the way just in time to avoid getting smacked.

Manchester United are famous now for never giving up, and know the damage such a late win can inflict on the other championship hopefuls. When it's you doing the winning, it makes you feel indestructible. But we've experienced the other side of the coin, too. One year under Jose Mourinho, Chelsea scored a succession of late goals and it definitely had an effect on us. No matter what people say, it gives you a stomach ache, it makes you feel sick – but it's an undeniable pleasure to inflict that on your rivals.

▼ It looks like I'm kicking Ole Gunnar Solskjaer up the backside as I nod in this goal against Chelsea at Old Trafford in January 2003, but the camera angle is deceptive. Actually I'm in plenty of space and David Beckham's cross, one of his wickedly curling specialities, has cleared Ole's head as he is challenged by William Gallas.

That day I was playing on the left and had drifted in at just the right moment to meet the delivery from the opposite flank. In fact, I jumped a bit too high and had to stoop slightly in mid-air to meet the ball. I caught it beautifully and it flashed past their keeper, Carlo Cudicini, and nestled in the corner. Very satisfying, especially as we went on to win 2–1, thanks to a late cracker from Diego Forlan.

▲ This was the aftermath of the scruffiest goal imaginable, the ball bouncing in off my shin after keeper Brad Friedel had spilled it and a defender had whacked it against me, but it got us out of jail in the first leg of our League Cup semi-final against Blackburn at Old Trafford in January 2003. We were awful that night, not even deserving the 1–1 draw that we got, and there is as much relief as triumph on the faces of Ruud van Nistelrooy and myself as we wheel away to celebrate.

That season was my most successful as a goalscorer – I managed twenty in all competitions – and a big part of the reason was that for much of the time I played up front with, or just behind, Ruud. Of course, he was the main man when it came to finding the net, and I felt I knew exactly what he wanted in terms of service; what runs he was going to make; when and where he wanted the ball delivered. He was an unbelievably efficient finisher who lived for goals and it was a joy to play with him. Mind, if he didn't score he'd sit in the back of the bus and sulk, even if we'd won the game. Then he'd look at the other results and if, say, Thierry Henry had scored then Ruud would be fuming even more. He perceived Henry as a personal rival and Ruud was adamant that *he* was going to get the most goals, all the time, even in training. I think that's a brilliant attitude from a centre forward and I wish they were all like that. Unquestionably, he would be top of my pile as an out-and-out finisher. The first time I saw him in training, my jaw dropped. We did shooting practice and he was completely ruthless.

I did a silly thing once which made Ruud mad. Away at Villa, someone headed the ball and it looked like it was going in. I just slid in to make sure but it turned out that Ruud was stood behind me, ready for a tap-in. He wasn't at all happy with me. I apologised for not seeing him but, in all honesty, I wouldn't have stepped aside even if I had noticed him. You can't say 'after you' in a game, even for the likes of Ruud van Nistelrooy.

▼ I equalised in the second leg of the League Cup semi-final at Blackburn, with a rather cleaner strike than my messy effort in the first leg. We needed this one because our old pal Andy Cole had put Rovers in front, but again I had a bit of luck because my first shot was blocked and the rebound sat up nicely for me to drive past Brad Friedel.

In the end we won 3–1 to reach Wembley, and I scored another which made it seven goals in six games, the most prolific sequence of my career. Of course, I'd been a centre forward from the age of eight until senior football so I already had the instinct for scoring, and it was an element of my game I was determined to keep when I moved back to midfield.

At this point I felt on top of the world with my confidence sky-high. The goals were a by-product, really, because when I was up front with Ruud I didn't think the main onus was on me to score, more to create opportunities for him. I'd try to find the holes, the room in which to work, then look for Ruud. That season he finished with forty-four goals, including a run of fifteen in ten games at the end, and I felt I had developed with him the same kind of understanding that I enjoyed with Ryan Giggs. Such chemistry is very, very precious in football.

◄ I can't think of any better way to spend a Saturday lunchtime than scoring a hat-trick in a beautiful stadium in front of some of the world's most passionate fans – and that's what happened to me at Newcastle as we stepped up our bid to regain the Premiership title in the spring of 2003. Though we won 6–2 in the end, we went behind early on to a cracker from Jermaine Jenas; then Ole Gunnar Solskjaer equalised before the script took a golden turn for me. Two minutes after Ole's goal, I played a one-two with him which set me up to volley us into the lead. Then another four minutes went by before some clever stuff between Ryan Giggs and Wes Brown teed me up on the edge of the box, and Olivier Bernard was too late to prevent my slightly sliced shot from flying into the top corner of Shay Given's net. Four minutes later, Ryan knocked in our fourth goal after John O'Shea had shivered the crossbar, and I completed my hat-trick with a tap-in early in the second half. Shortly afterwards, Ruud van Nistelrooy's penalty made it six goals in the space of twenty-six playing minutes, and Shola Ameobi's late consolation did nothing to take the gloss off one of our most devastating performances.

▼ I struck an unusually flamboyant pose as I celebrated the second hat-trick of my United career in front of our contingent of fabulously enthusiastic travelling fans at St James' Park. It's a good job Nicky Butt was closing in to bring me down to earth.

▲ If I'd missed this chance I would have been close to suicidal – that's if the lads hadn't murdered me anyway. It came with the score at 0–0 midway through the second half against Spurs at White Hart Lane, where we desperately needed to win to press home our advantage over Arsenal in the Premiership title race with only two more games to come.

Becks found me with a lovely pass, I flicked the ball out to Ryan on the left and continued into the box to meet his cross. There was plenty of pace on the delivery and all I had to do was nod it in from four or five yards. It wasn't one of those occasions when you shut your eyes and throw your head at the ball; it was just a case of a simple guided effort back across keeper Kasey Keller and into the massive space to his right.

Luckily I got it right, and there was a pretty impressive leap from Quinton Fortune, who was warming up on the far touchline, so involved with the action that he looks as if he's heading it in for us himself. Often when you see television shots of our bench, the manager can be caught doing that – and he never misses!

▼ Ruud van Nistelrooy appears to approve of my effort against Spurs, which just goes to show that he didn't have to score a goal himself to join in the celebrations with the team. He got another one at the end anyway, after a brilliant run from Quinton, so everybody was happy.

' *Paul and I had a very good connection together. He was always looking for me to make a run; he seemed to know where I was going and he could put the ball where it was necessary. I knew where he was going to turn and how he would deliver. He always had an eye for the killer pass and that suited me perfectly. As a striker it was wonderful to play with such a great provider. They don't come along very often. Paul was clever but uncomplicated – you knew what you were going to get from him, both on the field and off it.* '
RUUD VAN NISTELROOY

▲ I'm not usually one for community singing, but I was very happy to join in this particular refrain at Goodison. How did it go again? 'We've got our trophy back! We've got our trophy back! We've got our trophy back!' You get the idea . . . We'd only missed the one year of winning the Premiership after three titles on the trot, but that gap had hurt us badly. All season the fans had been chanting that they *wanted* it back; now we could sing that we had *got* it back.

There was nothing riding on the last game, but we won it anyway by two goals to one. I don't think the Everton players were happy with our winner, a penalty earned by Ruud and converted by him. Certainly they weren't the most hospitable people that day. Did that dampen our celebrations? Well, does it look like it?

▲ The champagne is still dripping down my face as I nurse the Premiership trophy in the Goodison Park dressing room, after the presentation on the final day of the 2002/03 season. Who did I have to worry about most when the bubbly was being squirted? Everybody was at it, but probably it wasn't a bad idea to steer clear of Nicky Butt and Roy Keane. They were both expert enough to get you between the eyes from a dozen paces. It was absolute bedlam, but believe me, nobody was complaining.

▼ This is me pondering a future career in public relations . . . yeah, right! Given the way I am widely perceived as being private and shy of publicity, this shot might amuse a few people. But actually all I was trying to do was keep warm on the bench at Old Trafford. It can be freezing sometimes when you're stuck in the dugout for all or most of a match. We don't have heated seats, either, or hot-water bottles like those delicate flowers at Manchester City. To be fair, our club coats are pretty good; it's your feet you have to worry about. It's not much good being called on as a sub, then trying to kick a football with blocks of ice.

In reality, I'm not shrinking away from the camera. That's the last thing on my mind. All I'm thinking about is the game and what contribution I can make if the manager calls me on. It can be the hardest thing in the world to be plunged into the action after freezing for an hour. One minute you're sat on the bench, the next you're sprinting all over the pitch, and sometimes it can be difficult to catch your breath. Perhaps those hot-water bottles aren't such a bad idea after all . . .

9

2003/04

CONSOLATION IN CARDIFF

Though some Manchester United fans might describe any season in which we don't take the title as a disappointment, we have no divine right to the big prize and we could only applaud Arsenal's incredible achievement of not losing a single League game while taking it from us in 2003/04. They were our main Premiership rivals down the years, and I know we don't like 'em, but this time, they deserved their reward. Sure, they had a bit of luck at Old Trafford when Ruud hit the bar with a late penalty which would have won the game for us, but they were a powerful, well-balanced team and worthy champions. I can't deny that we were devastated to finish fifteen points behind them in third place, although our victory over Henry, Vieira and company in an FA Cup semi-final offered some balm to our wounds.

When we beat Millwall in the FA Cup final it earned me my third winner's medal in the famous old competition which, sadly, has become a little bit devalued in recent years compared to its sky-high status in the old days.

▲ It was a proud moment for myself, Ryan Giggs and Gary Neville when we were voted into the Premiership team of the decade back in August 2003. We saw it as a really significant tribute to be recognised as three of the better players in the League over such a long time span. Of course, none of us would have dreamed that we'd all still be playing for Manchester United eight seasons down the line, when we had a collective age of more than a century! That is downright amazing.

❛ *Paul is absolutely the most talented footballer I've ever played with and I consider myself blessed to have been his teammate. It's not just me who rates him so highly. People like Zidane, Xavi, Vieira, Petit, Davids, they've all said that Paul is the best they've faced, and they're the people who should know. Every day for the last fifteen or twenty years we have played possession football in training, and you can bet your life that if Paul is on your team you'll win the session. He controls the entire routine, the tempo of the whole exercise. It's as though he has eyes in the back of his head because he knows where everybody is all the time. He has a level of intelligence on the football pitch which I don't think I've ever seen in anyone else – and I've seen a few.* ❜

GARY NEVILLE

➤ Both Seba Veron and myself are looking a trifle apprehensive here, as if we'd been told to jump into the ring to slug it out for a central midfield role, but I don't think our manager would be that cruel. We were just going through a pre-season boxing exercise to improve our all-round sharpness. It's an unbelievable sport; I really don't know how boxers can throw so many punches. I only worked out for thirty seconds, a minute at the most, by hitting a padded glove and I was totally knackered at the end of it.

Seba was a sensational footballing talent but he did cause me a bit of a problem when he arrived in 2001 because for quite a few games I was shifted from central to left midfield. Looking back, I think I made it more of a problem than I should have done. I should have concentrated on my game rather than worrying about the new man. But United had paid nearly £30 million for him and it was in my head that I might miss out. I was up for negotiating a new contract at that point and it even crossed my mind that it might be time for me to go somewhere else. Not that I wanted to, but I was twenty-seven going on twenty-eight, and I wanted to be sure of playing regularly.

Really, it doesn't matter who comes into a team. If you're playing well enough then you'll be in the side, that's always the way the manager operates and that's completely fair. As it turned out, I did okay on the left, scoring a few goals, but I never relished it. I definitely preferred the middle to shuttling up and down the wing.

As a lad, Seba was lovely, I got on really well with him as I always seem to do with South Americans. It was the same with Gabby Heinze, Diego Forlan, Carlos Tevez – they didn't have much English so we didn't talk a lot, which might be what we had in common! As a footballer, the English style of play didn't quite work out for Seba, though there were times when he was devastating on the pitch. Maybe the lifestyle didn't suit him – certainly the change in weather would have been a novelty.

◄ Chewing the fat with Nicky Butt, one of my best friends in football, during a break in training at Carrington. No doubt he's taking the mick out of somebody here. Butty is the funniest lad I've ever met – there are times when he has you aching with laughter. He can make a joke out of anything and the only pity is that you can't repeat most of the stories!

I'd known him for years before we came to United, having played with him for a team in Oldham called Boundary Park, and then we came through the Old Trafford youth system together. We became really close, often going on holiday together along with our respective girlfriends at the time.

At every stage of his development Nicky was an exceptional footballer, one for the rest of us to look up to because he was the first one from our year to make an impact in the first team. He was such a physical player that stepping up to confront men was no problem for him.

In the summer of 1995, when Paul Ince left the club, the fans were understandably anxious, but the manager knew that he had this exceptional youngster up his sleeve and that he would be capable of stepping into the breach. That's a measure of how outstanding Nicky was, because Paul was a truly top-class performer.

Obviously Nicky and I don't see as much of each other now that he's left United, but often we talk on the phone. We still own a racehorse together and we'll always be mates.

▼ My old United pal Henning Berg and I found ourselves on opposite sides when Manchester United and Rangers were drawn together during the Champions League group stage in the autumn of 2003. I am doing the splits while Henning takes a breather here at Ibrox – neither of us has control of the ball and the whole night was a bit like that. Feverish, you might call it, with the atmosphere really crackling. Unquestionably, Rangers represented a tough test. In the end we won by the game's only goal, contributed early on by Phil Neville – one of his rare hits.

It was good to catch up with Henning, who was a terrific defender in his pomp and a nice lad. By this time he was coming towards the end of his career and he had adopted the fashion of shaving his head. Whether that was because his hair was falling out anyway, I wouldn't like to say . . .

▲ It's hard to imagine a better feeling than scoring in a Manchester derby and I was lucky enough to experience it a couple of times when City visited us in December 2003. We won the game 3–1 and this photo shows our opener after seven minutes, when Gary Neville bombed down the right touchline and his delivery reached me at just the right moment. Gary was brilliant at whipping in his crosses and my job was to anticipate where they were going so that I could get to them before the defenders.

It's very difficult marking a midfielder who arrives late in the box, and particularly in the early and middle parts of my career I managed to collect quite a few goals by popping up in space, such as in this instance, where I'm free several yards away from City centre half Richard Dunne. As a midfielder, although you don't get as many scoring chances, often they are easier to put away than those that fall the way of a centre forward, who tends to be more heavily marked. Inevitably, as I grew older I found it harder to arrive late in the box after a sprint from midfield, but it was still supremely satisfying when it happened.

In this game we seemed to be comfortable after Ruud van Nistelrooy added to my early effort, but then Shaun Wright-Phillips, who can be glimpsed in the background of this picture, pulled one back and I was relieved to nod in our third, courtesy of a cross from Kleberson. It was nice, too, that my former England teammate David Seaman was the man picking the ball out of the net. I didn't put many past him, so this felt special.

◀ Here is another of those scrambled goals that I seem to have accumulated during my career, this time after narrowly beating Manchester City's Icelandic keeper Arni Arason to a cross from Ryan Giggs and prodding the ball over the line with my shin. It was the opener in a 4–2 home win which put us into the quarter-finals of the

FA Cup, a particularly impressive result as we were reduced to ten men for more than half the match after Gary Neville was sent off for clashing with Steve McManaman. Even though they were England teammates, it's fair to say that the pair of them never got on too well together.

This time, Gary was reckoned to have headbutted McManaman over a penalty appeal, an action which was totally out of character for him. However, if City thought we were going to cave in because we went down to ten men, they had another

think coming. Having a man sent off, particularly if you perceive there has been an injustice — as in this case, when Gary was accused spuriously of having dived before the confrontation — it can make the depleted side fight a little bit harder, and that happened here. We were one up when Gary was dismissed and we stretched that to four, which is remarkable for ten men, before City came back with two late on. They had about 10,000 fans in and our crowd got right behind us, so the atmosphere was electric. It was a great day for us and miserable for City, which is just the way we like it.

➤ If my grin was any wider after that scruffy effort, my head would have fallen in half! I know it wasn't the greatest strike, but so what? A goal's a goal, no matter how it comes, and this brought me just as much joy as any thirty-yarder — maybe more, judging from the look on my face!

▲ First, the good news from the dramatic night of Jose Mourinho's first visit to Old Trafford, as the boss of Porto in the second leg of our Champions League last-sixteen clash in the spring of 2004. We were 2–1 down from the first leg, but after half an hour I was able to wipe out the deficit with this glancing header from a pinpoint cross from the left by John O'Shea. He was having a fabulous season at left-back and this delivery was typical of his excellent service. I reached the ball just ahead of Nicky Butt, who would have shouted if he'd thought he was in a better position than me to score, but he realised Sheasy's knock was dropping perfectly for me.

▶ Now for the bad news . . . Soon after our aggregate equaliser, Sheasy and I combined again to fashion a perfectly good goal but I was given offside, a decision which television replays showed to be woefully incorrect. Sheasy got the ball on the left of the box and drove in a shot-cum-cross which I managed to control, then poke past the Portuguese keeper Vitor Baia with my second touch. As I turned towards goal I was certain I was onside, but when I looked across I was shattered to see the linesman had raised his flag. We were well on top at the time and I am convinced this would have been the clincher had it been allowed to stand.

Later, they scored to win the tie at the very death, which set Mourinho cavorting down the touchline in his famous dance. It was the first time we had really become aware of him and it signalled the start of his high profile. It was annoying to watch, but we could understand his reaction because he was so happy for his team.

As for us, we were absolutely devastated because we didn't get what we deserved in a massively important game. Still, you have to take a philosophical view. Down the years I'm sure I've been given goals which should have been flagged offside, so I have to accept that the rub of the green went against me on this occasion. Even at the time, there's no point in dwelling on the injustice. You have to put it to bed straight away because there's always another game coming up fast. I've never been one to agonise in front of a video afterwards. The incident is gone, so what's the point?

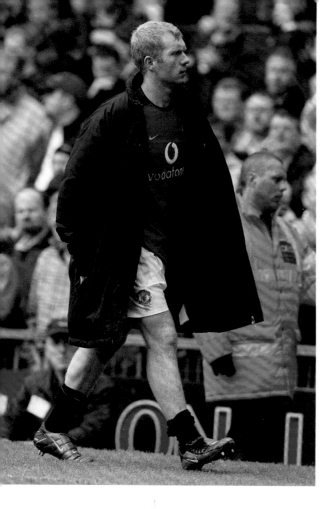

◄ I don't look too happy about being substituted ten minutes before half-time against Chelsea at Old Trafford in May 2004, but I had to console myself with the thought that the manager had a very good reason. I'd been booked for some silly misdemeanour and if I'd picked up another card I would have been suspended for the FA Cup final a couple of weeks later, so the disconsolate expression is partly because I was feeling a little bit stupid and frustrated with myself.

Of course, it is still hard to take leaving the action with so much football still to be played, but the boss is there to manage his players and that's what he was doing. Would I ever have been tempted to start a debate with him over that sort of decision? Not a chance. There were those who might have, but never me. I'd like to think I had more sense!

◄ This is the goal that gave us some measure of revenge for Arsenal winning the League in 2003/04 without losing a single game. We had to stand back and give them credit for a fantastic achievement, but it hurt us like hell, so beating them 1–0 in the semi-final of the FA Cup at Villa Park was extremely sweet.

It was a decent goal, too. When Gary Neville found Ryan Giggs on the right – God knows what he was doing there – I was running through the middle and shouted for the ball. Ryan gave me a perfect pass and I just put my right foot through it from about twenty yards without breaking stride. I didn't aim for any particular part of the goal, just concentrated on hitting it as cleanly and as hard as I could. Somehow the flight deceived Jens Lehmann and he ended up diving out of the way, so the ball hit the net right where he'd been standing.

We owed a lot to our keeper, Roy Carroll, who made a series of exceptional saves early in the game, and to Darren Fletcher, who put in a remarkably mature

display in midfield for a lad only just out of his teens, never giving an inch against the formidable Patrick Vieira.

With all due respect to the other semi-finalists, Millwall and Sunderland, it did feel a bit like winning the FA Cup that sunny day in Birmingham because both of them were in the division below us. They might have beaten us, of course, but we knew that with Arsenal out of the way we were in with a colossal chance of taking the trophy.

'*For me as a midfielder, Paul Scholes was the best possible teacher. When people ask me my hardest opponent, I always refer to Paul in training. Facing him improved me so much because his astonishing quality gave me something to aim for. He never gave the ball away, he could nutmeg you, he could make you look a fool, his range of passing was remarkable, his touch and awareness, everything was top notch. Seeing Scholesy made you stand back and realise you had a long way to go, because he was awesome.*'

DARREN FLETCHER

▼ There is barely a player I've encountered during my lifetime in football who hasn't struck me as a fundamentally decent bloke, but one I've got absolutely no time for is Dennis Wise, seen here tangling with me during United's FA Cup final victory over Millwall in 2004.

For my taste he spent too much time committing niggly fouls and trying to get inside people's minds. That approach might work with some opponents, but he was wasting his time by trying it on us.

At his peak he was a fine player brimming with talent, able to pick a pass, take a free kick, score a goal. Wise could play the game all right, but I could never stomach his attitude.

When we met at Cardiff he was well past his peak, and Millwall never really threatened us on our way to a 3–0 victory.

▲ Giggsy made the most of the opportunity to flash his hairy chest while I remained the model of decorum by retaining my shirt as we celebrated in the Millennium dressing room after beating Millwall in the 2004 FA Cup final. It's always a hectic scene after such a big match, with our resident snapper, John Peters, nipping around to make sure he gets a decent shot of everyone with the cup. Much as we'd like to, Manchester United can't win the Premiership title every year, but the oldest trophy in the professional game still represents a fair old consolation.

▼ I'm far more comfortable in casual gear than putting on the gladrags for a formal event, but it doesn't happen too often – perhaps two or three times a year – so I haven't got much to complain about. After all, my wife, Claire, comes with me and she likes getting dressed up, so it's only fair to make a bit of an effort, especially as it's usually for a very good cause. United are heavily involved in UNICEF, which does so much wonderful work for children and mothers in developing countries, and if I can do some little thing to help – perhaps by donating something to be auctioned, and maybe buying something, too – then I'm only too willing. Apart from anything else it's a good night out, and the dicky bow doesn't tend to last the whole evening.

10

ENGLAND
2002–2004

AN AGONISING
DECISION

If the second half of my England career had gone as well as the first, then it would have been considerably more difficult for me to withdraw from international football, which I did after the European Championship in Portugal in the summer of 2004.

At the end of this chapter I deal with my reason for stepping aside after sixty-six caps at the age of twenty-nine, but I'll mention here that the pundits who speculated that my international retirement was down to unhappiness with the way I was deployed by manager Sven-Goran Eriksson were a long way off the mark. I want to be clear that I wasn't rejecting either my country or the man in charge – it was a lot more personal than that.

▲ I always enjoyed a spot of synchronised formation dancing with Phil Neville during training because he's such a lovely little mover, although for some reason the other England lads don't seem to be giving us their undivided attention in this photo. Phil likes a bit of a dance, he's a natural, especially after a glass or two of pink champagne. Not like me. I have to be very drunk to get up and venture on to the dance floor. What if Phil gives me some lessons? Er, I think I'll pass on that . . .

❛ Despite Paul's generous words, I'm not the most enthusiastic of dancers, though it's true that a bit of the pink stuff can make a difference. As to lessons, that won't happen any time soon, though I can confirm that my sense of rhythm is slightly more developed than Paul's. ❜

PHIL NEVILLE

▼ It won't surprise anyone to learn that David Beckham and I have never used the same hairdresser. This was one of his more extravagant styles – in fact, I'm not completely sure whether it's Becks or Robbie Savage. Becks was always amazing with his hairdos; it seemed like there was something new every week. It kept me well entertained because I never knew what fantastic creation was coming next; it was brilliant. The special moment was always the 'big reveal' when the hat came off. It was like the curtains opening on a work of art – or something like that! Did the other lads take the mick? Probably we did the first couple of times, but then we got used to it. It was all part of him.

I have to admit I was never tempted to follow suit. I never had the hair for it, never been one for putting on the gel, never even bothered about having a hairstyle. Nothing's changed now, obviously! There are people who reckon I should be a bit more fashion-conscious, or at least a bit more tidy. But I can't be bothered, and I'm too old to change now.

◄ One of the best two or three footballers I have ever seen was Zinedine Zidane. Here I am striving to keep up with him during England's 2–1 defeat by France in our Euro 2004 opener in Lisbon, in which the great man scored both their goals during stoppage time.

Zidane has made some very complimentary remarks about me in recent times. I hesitate to repeat them, but he called me the complete midfielder and his toughest opponent, which I have to confess left me pretty well flabbergasted. I mean, to have a player of his calibre saying anything at all about me is wonderful, but to read such generous words from such a master of the game is truly awesome. To see Zidane in action was to witness poetry in motion. The skills, the vision, the goals . . . he was a sublime performer. When he was at his peak, winning the World Cup, the Champions League and all the rest, he was unquestionably the finest player on the planet.

▼ I'll make no bones about it, I wasn't satisfied with my form during Euro 2004 in Portugal, not even in the 3–0 win over Switzerland in our second game, and it came as a huge relief when I scored this goal in the next one, against Croatia. That it was my first in thirty appearances for England speaks volumes. As a central midfielder I should have been doing far better than that, and even though people kindly assured me that I was still contributing in other ways, I was far from happy. I always try to be honest. I'm a perfectionist, very self-critical, always have been and always will be, and I can't deny that my level of performance was a factor in my imminent decision to retire from international football.

This was only a messy little header after some tremendous work by Wayne Rooney had set me up, but it put us level at 1–1 and we went on to win 4–2, which qualified us to meet Portugal in the quarter-finals. It proved to be my last goal and my penultimate appearance for England.

▼ The end is nigh for my England career which, I'm sorry to say, finished on a low note when we lost on penalties to Portugal in the quarter-finals of Euro 2004 in Lisbon. The flat-out David Beckham is inconsolable, while I'm still vertical but decidedly glum.

◄ It's high time I explained the most controversial act of my football career, my decision to give up playing for England back in 2004. A lot of people reckoned at the time it was because I had a grudge against the manager, Sven-Goran Eriksson, for playing me wide on the left instead of in my preferred role of central midfield. In fact, nothing could be further from the truth. After all, often I was used on the left for United and did well there.

Let me emphasise now that I thought the world of Sven. He was so relaxed and that mood transferred to the team. He didn't say a lot, but then he didn't have to. There were no complications about his approach, he just told us to express ourselves within a straight four-four-two. Socially, he treated us as adults; if you wanted a glass of wine the night before a game, that was fine. And I do believe that he did well for England, taking us to the quarter-finals of the World Cup, which probably reflected our true level. Overall, he was a really nice man who trusted his players and championed exactly the sort of entertaining football I enjoy.

In fact, the main reason I retired from internationals at the age of twenty-nine was extremely simple – I never liked being away from my home and my family for weeks on end. Whenever England went away for a tournament, I was okay for maybe the first three or four days, but after that I was unhappy because I was missing my wife and children.

People are different; I wouldn't expect anyone else to feel the same way, but that's how I happen to be. Whenever we were knocked out I was always more than ready to go home, even though it might seem like sacrilege to say such a thing, and certainly I mean no disrespect to the fans who save their money to travel all over the world watching England. Given my mindset, I never enjoyed the football, and therefore had no chance of being anywhere near my best. As a result my form and overall contribution were not up to scratch. Clearly that was not a tenable situation for anyone concerned, which is why I put an end to it. A secondary factor in my disenchantment with the England set-up was the selfish attitude of some other players. Like all the United lads, I wanted to be part of a team, but there were too many individuals who appeared to be there for personal glory. I felt they didn't care enough about England, that they were using the national team as a way to be noticed, perhaps to secure a move to a bigger club. I found that very frustrating.

I made up my mind to retire on my own, then informed Sir Alex, who told me to go with how I felt. There was never any question, as has been suggested, of attempting to prolong my club days by quitting England. As for Sven, he thought I was crazy to be giving away my international career at such a young age, but he wasn't going to stand in my way. To me, it was like a huge burden being lifted from my shoulders.

In future I could look forward to summertime without that sense of foreboding which had preyed on me for so long. I had made the right decision for my family and myself, and since then I have never felt otherwise.

Yes, I was tempted when Steve McClaren asked me to reconsider, but visions of being away from home all summer once again put me off. Then in 2010 I was approached first by Stuart Pearce, then Fabio Capello's assistant Franco Baldini, about joining the squad for the World Cup in South Africa. I told myself I wouldn't face the same pressure to score goals at that stage of my career, and again I pondered hard, but with the same result. I suppose I might have felt a bit more wanted if Capello had phoned me personally – certainly United's manager wouldn't leave a call like that to his assistants – but frankly I doubt if it would have made any difference. Anyway, I was given only a day to make up my mind, which was not enough, and if there was the slightest tinge of regret when I was sat at home watching the World Cup on television, it had no lasting effect on me. It was gone, water under the bridge; I could cope with it.

Apart from feeling awkward about taking the place of somebody who had travelled all over the place in the qualifying competition, I had thought about my family – and that was more than enough for me.

' *Paul finished with the national team too early, in my opinion, but he is a family man and you have to respect that. He was always a delight to work with, educated, polite, very quiet. I never had the hint of a problem with him. As a footballer, he was one of the best I ever worked with. I would have loved to have had him with me when he was sixteen with his whole career before him. He was magnificent; very clever with outstanding technique. He could pass the ball over five yards or fifty; he could see things to set up other people; he could shoot and he could score goals.*

If you gave me Paul Scholes and ten others, I would be happy. I would tell them to give him the ball and then we would have a good team. '

SVEN-GORAN ERIKSSON

11

2004/05, 2005/06

BETWEEN SUMMITS

With Wayne Rooney bedding in so brilliantly at Old Trafford after his arrival from Everton, and Cristiano Ronaldo beginning to emerge as one of the best players in the world, 2004/05 and 2005/06 was a period of positive transition for Manchester United, even though we were helpless to prevent Jose Mourinho's Chelsea from winning back-to-back Premiership titles.

In 2004/05, we slipped to third place in the table and this time we also missed out on an FA Cup consolation when I goofed up in the penalty shoot-out at the Millennium to present the trophy to Arsenal, whom we had outplayed comprehensively during the actual game. A season later we improved to take the runners-up slot in the League and, despite the exit of the colossally influential Roy Keane, I felt that once again we had the makings of a Premiership-winning side. I scored fewer goals than in any previous campaign, but that was partly due to a debilitating eye condition which had me on the sidelines for four months. With that sorted by the season's end, I was raring to go again.

◄ I do look a trifle knackered in this snap from United's 2004 Community Shield defeat by Arsenal, but the shooting action appears to be in decent working order and the body is lean – indicating that I must have looked after myself properly in the recent summer which has, as always, turned my hair blond. Perhaps it's just the natural expression of a man with his thirtieth birthday on the horizon and another long season in prospect.

▲ 'If you don't give me that free kick then I'm going home and I'm taking my ball with me!' It was nothing quite as drastic as that, but I do look a bit peeved with a decision down at Chelsea on the opening day of the 2004/05 Premiership season. No doubt I was in a bad mood because we played well enough to win the game, but lost it to a rather lucky goal by Eidur Gudjohnsen.

▼ It was weird playing against Nicky Butt for the first time in our professional lives following his transfer to Newcastle in the summer of 2004. Knowing him so well for so long, I was as familiar with his game as my own and it was hard to get my mind round the fact that he was playing for the opposition when we walked out at St James' Park for this encounter that November.

Beforehand we had a little smile together about the strangeness of the situation but once we were into the action it was no longer an issue. At that point you just get on with it, there can't be any friendliness between you then. During the game I made it my business to be aware of Nicky's whereabouts all the time because he is such a marvellous tackler and all-round footballer that I could have been outdone. As it turned out, there were no particular collisions between us and we won 3–1, so I was the happier man afterwards.

I was gutted personally when Nicky left Old Trafford because we had been together for so long, but United is a gigantic club where people come and go all the time and you just have to get on with it. You have to realise that however good a player is, he'll always be replaced in the end. Nicky had made his mind up that he wanted to be where he would play a lot more football than he was doing at Old Trafford, and I had to respect his decision.

▼ I think it's the manager's main aim in his press conferences to wind people up, and usually his victim is a journalist or the boss of another club. Just occasionally, though, it might happen to be one of his own players, and this time I drew the short straw. I hated facing the massed ranks of the media, but the club is obliged to roll out a player along with the manager ahead of European games, so I had to grit my teeth and get on with it once in a while. Mind, if you want to learn how to handle the press, there's no better teacher than Sir Alex Ferguson.

Obviously the manager has to respond to questions, but I'm sure he plans the main thrust of what he's going to say beforehand. When I've been waiting with him ahead of a conference, it's been clear that he relishes the cut and thrust. Sometimes he might even say, 'Watch this.' Then you sit back and witness the master at work. It doesn't matter what the issues are, he's always in control. Of course, he's in control of the entire club, has been for years, and you might say he's the ultimate control freak. Whatever he says goes and he's earned that over the years with all the success he's enjoyed. In terms of handling the press, he could write the book, and nothing fazes him. He's at Manchester United where there are big stories all the time, but to him big stories are nothing. The press never have anything new to throw at him. He knows absolutely everything that's going on; he's ready for anything and I think he always will be.

▲ If you're going to suffer a goal-scoring drought – and it's not much fun, believe me – then I guess this wasn't a bad way to come out the other side. We were at home to Charlton late in November 2004 and I hadn't found the net all season. Worse than that, I wasn't happy with my all-round game. Maybe it was a vicious circle, with my confidence dropping because of the lack of goals. I know that scoring doesn't necessarily define my entire contribution, but to me it was always an integral part of what I had to offer. Without those precious goals I had always been able to deliver, I was struggling more than at any previous time in my career, and I began to get a bit of stick from the media, quite understandably.

But salvation was at hand. I was hovering near Charlton's back post when Darren Fletcher slung over a cross from the right and the ball arrived in the perfect slot for an aerial volley. I caught it sweetly and, luckily for me, it flew past their keeper Dean Kiely into the net, sealing our 2–0 victory. I'd have been delighted to get any old sort of goal, it could have been off my backside for all I cared, but it was nice to break my duck with a little bit of a flourish. Cheers, Fletch!

◄ The relief at scoring a goal at last is showing clearly on my face as Ryan Giggs arrives for the celebration. When anyone goes through the sort of nightmare patch I was experiencing, naturally the other players are aware of it and anxious for it to end, and Giggsy was clearly extra pleased on my behalf. Everybody pulling together is a big part of what being in a team is about, and he typifies that. Mind, he was probably thinking, 'About bloody time!' And I couldn't blame him.

Had I felt that I might be on the way out of United if I couldn't stop the rot? No, because the manager kept picking me. He always maintained his confidence in me. I kept thinking, even as I drove to a game, that today was sure to be the day I was left out. But he always stuck by me and in the end I came good.

' *For a player of Scholesy's quality, it was only ever going to be a matter of time before his drought ended. I was certain that once he had scored one then he would go on a run – and he did. In such a situation it's natural that you worry and get a bit uptight. You try everything – new boots, different superstitions, the lot – but in the end it comes down to having faith in your ability.* '

RYAN GIGGS

▼ After the famine, then came the feast. Having not scored for months, then finally lifting the monkey off my back by knocking that one in against Charlton, the goals just kept on coming – seven of them in a sequence of seven games.

This is the first of my pair in our 3–0 win over West Bromwich Albion at the Hawthorns in November and the way it happened was typical of my complete change of fortune. I was carrying the ball forward and just as I came within shooting range it sat up perfectly for me to hit it, and it flew into the corner of their net. A few matches earlier, most likely it would have bobbled at the crucial moment and I'd have hit the corner flag. Judging from the slightly sceptical expression on the face of Roy Keane, running alongside me, perhaps that's what he expected to happen.

Now the pressure was lifted, instead of being tense ahead of games I was relaxed, and everything fell into place.

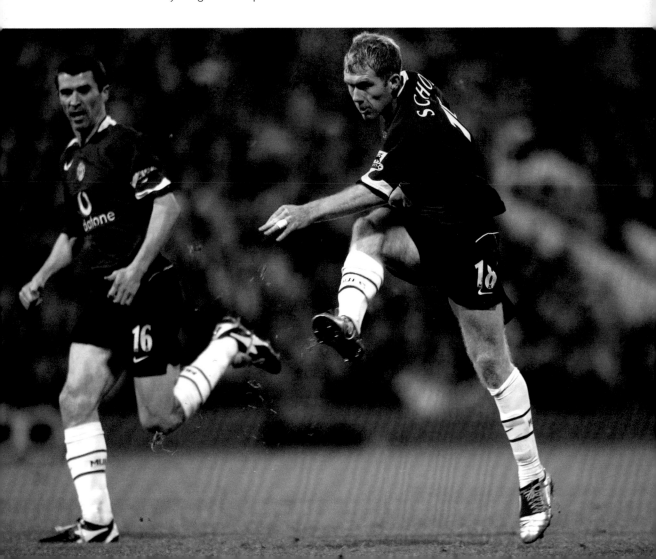

▲ Anything Wayne Rooney can do . . . I'm joking, of course. I don't think I'm quite as far off the ground as Wayne was when he scored that wonder goal to beat Manchester City at Old Trafford in February 2011 – not by several feet, actually! Another difference is that his shot finished up in the net, whereas I can't recall what happened to my effort at home to Crystal Palace some six seasons earlier, only that it didn't bring us a goal.

The overhead kick isn't something I ever practised. It's a specialist skill and if someone is good at it, it's amazing how often the ball arrives in the right area for them to attempt it. You have to make a split-second decision to try it when the ball comes in and you can't reach it in any other way. I'm told that Denis Law was brilliant at overheads and bicycle kicks, but the one from my time that stands out is Mark Hughes, who put away some absolute crackers. As for me, I haven't put one away since my schooldays. I did score a couple of goals in this 5–2 victory over Palace, but they weren't spectacular, I'm afraid.

▲ Battling for possession with Mr AC Milan, Paolo Maldini, one of the all-time greats of world football, in the last sixteen of the Champions League at Old Trafford in February 2005. He reminds me of Ryan Giggs in many ways because he played all his football for one leading club, starting at the age of seventeen and not finishing till he was forty. I can see Ryan doing that, no problem. Milan are similar to United in that they value their home-grown players highly and keep lots of them into their late thirties. It says a lot for their methods that so many last so long.

Like Ryan, Maldini was never just along for the ride. At the time of this encounter, which we sadly lost 1–0 on the night and 2–0 on aggregate, Maldini was thirty-six but still a formidable force, quick and skilful, strong and athletic. A couple of seasons later I saw him face up to Cristiano Ronaldo, who was getting better all the time but just couldn't figure out a way to get past the Italian. Maldini was top-notch to the end. Any club in the world would have wanted him, but he was a Milan man and that was it and all about it.

➤ I am a firm believer that professional footballers should always go to acknowledge their fans at the end of a game, no matter what the result. We might feel embarrassed because we've put in a rotten performance, but the least we can do is show a bit of appreciation, especially when we're away from home, and people have travelled a long way to see us.

On this occasion, in March 2005, it was easy, because I'd scored a couple in a 4–0 FA Cup win at Southampton, and the supporters were celebrating. Still, they had shown devotion above and beyond the call of duty by going all the way down to the south coast, especially as they must have been horribly disappointed by our shocking display in losing to Milan only four days earlier.

When we're on the road, our fans are always brilliant. They'll travel anywhere to see us, sometimes even amazing us by turning up for a pre-season game in Hong Kong or Japan. In England and in Europe they'll fill every available seat, even though it can be very difficult and horrendously expensive to come by tickets. From the moment we step on to the pitch the fans are singing and it gives us a huge lift to have such passionate backing at every match. They're the best, and their loyalty means the world to us.

▲ This glancing header from an exquisitely flighted Cristiano Ronaldo cross put us two in front against Newcastle in our 2005 FA Cup semi-final at the Millennium. Coming on the stroke of half-time as it did, it must have been a devastating blow to our opponents.

Semi-finals can be tense affairs, but this was comfortable for us in the end, with Ruud van Nistelrooy scoring twice and Cristiano once to seal a 4–1 victory. On the losing side was my old mate Nicky Butt. I felt for him, but that would have been scant consolation to a player who was desperate to win every time he walked on to a pitch.

▼ Training's not all serious, we do have a laugh – pretty often actually. Of course, we know how to get down to business, but football has to be fun, too. Here something has tickled me so much that I'm on the verge of falling over, while Roy Keane seems to find it funnier than Wes Brown. What provoked the guffaws? It's almost inevitably to do with Wayne Rooney, who will have got up to some sort of nonsense, probably an antic from the Nicky Butt school of daftness.

Roy was always a top trainer, but he knew how to take the mick out of the other players as well. As the skipper he was very much our leader, and he knew a bit of fun was good for team spirit. What about Wesley? It would be an exaggeration to say he loves to train, but you can always guarantee that he'll be 100 per cent ready when matchday comes around. He's a terrific character, a local boy and a tough and classy defender who has done magnificently to achieve so much in the face of so many horrendous injuries. I wish him all the best for his new challenge at Sunderland.

▼ Turning away from young Master Fabregas, only recently turned eighteen, during our FA Cup final against Arsenal at the Millennium in May 2005. It was apparent even then that he was a terrific player, but if I'm honest, I didn't envisage him progressing quite the way he has. Arsene Wenger, seeing him every day, obviously knew that he had something special, and so it's proved.

That said, he didn't have a profound influence on this game, which we should have won with plenty to spare. We battered them for ninety minutes, then ran them ragged in extra time, and we created chance after chance but couldn't take any of them. Ruud van Nistelrooy hit the bar when it seemed a certainty he must score and I missed a couple of opportunities which haunt me to this day. I just don't know how we didn't win.

▲ In the end, it was my fault that we didn't take the FA Cup home to Manchester. Ten people took penalties during that dramatic Millennium showdown and only one missed – me! Spot-kicks have never been my strength, although I did score from one in the Community Shield shoot-out against the same opponents at the start of the previous season. This time I was second up after Ruud had tucked away our opener. In truth, it wasn't a great effort. I telegraphed where it was going and it was the perfect height for Jens Lehmann to make the save, diving to his right.

At that point it wasn't all over, of course, and I was praying that Arsenal would cock one up, but they never did. When Patrick Vieira scored the winner I was utterly devastated. The fact that we had dominated the game made me feel worse than if we'd been outplayed. Seeing Arsenal celebrate was overwhelmingly galling; it makes me shudder even now.

My wife and kids were there, and I wondered what they were thinking – probably that I shouldn't have been trusted to take a penalty. But I was asked if I fancied one and I said yes. Doh!

I felt that I had let the team down. I don't know if the other lads blamed me, only they can say that, but I know I wouldn't blame anybody in similar circumstances. I'd take the view that at least he'd been brave enough to have a go, but I would say that, wouldn't I? I don't think the manager allowed me to take one afterwards and I could understand why.

Yet despite my Cardiff agony, I do think a penalty shoot-out is a suitable method for settling a game if the scores are level after 120 minutes. It's so exciting, fantastic drama, and I always enjoy watching one when I'm not involved. In the old days a tie might run to four or five replays, but that could get boring, and the expense for the fans nowadays would be astronomical. I think you'd be lucky to end up with half a crowd.

◄ The future's bright; the future's Red. I couldn't have been happier sitting down with Manchester United chief executive David Gill to sign my last long contract with the club in August 2005. That took me up to 2009, after which I put pen to paper on one-year deals.

I always wanted security at Old Trafford because I never had the slightest desire to go anywhere else. If the club had wanted to sell me then I would have had to face a move, but it would have been an almighty and unwelcome wrench.

At this point, I was coming up to thirty-one, so it was a huge commitment from United because you can't be certain how quickly you are going to age at this stage of your career. That said, they could be sure I had looked after myself physically, they knew my character, and obviously the manager estimated that I'd still be able to do a decent job for him in my middle thirties. I hope I proved him right.

I always got on well with David Gill, who is a nice guy, very fair and a straight talker. He knows his football, too, which helps. His lad, Ollie, is currently coming through the United ranks as a centre half or left-back. He's tall like his dad, a left-footer, and I'd expect him to be challenging for a place in the first-team squad before too long. Ollie's a good player and he's definitely got a chance.

► Tussling for possession with my old United pal Diego Forlan during our goalless draw with Villarreal in Spain in September 2005 was a challenge because he was playing so well. Diego didn't enjoy the greatest of times at Old Trafford, though he'll always be remembered for his two goals when we won at Liverpool, a couple of terrific efforts against Chelsea and a cracker against Rangers, too. So it wasn't all bad for him in Manchester, but you would never have guessed how brilliantly he would fare after moving to Spain.

I think the English lifestyle, and particularly the weather in our part of the world, wasn't really for Diego. Like so many South Americans who come to these shores, he missed the Latin culture. You don't see many of them thriving in England or staying for long, though I hope our Brazilians – Anderson and the Da Silva twins, Rafael and Fabio – prove to be exceptions.

Diego was a really nice lad who never complained, and who tried his best to make it work at Old Trafford, but clearly he was in the wrong place. We knew he had quality as a footballer but I have to admit it's surprised everybody how phenomenally well he's done since leaving United. Twice he's won the Golden Boot award as the top scorer in Europe, first with Villarreal and then with Atletico Madrid, and he was voted the best player in the 2010 World Cup. Wow, that's some achievement!

This game saw one of my rare excursions into captaincy – if you look closely you'll spot the armband, somewhat camouflaged by Diego's strip – but I've never relished the role, as I'll explain later.

▲ 'A word in your ear!' The manager gives me my instructions as I prepare to take the pitch as a substitute for Ruud van Nistelrooy after eighty-three minutes at Fulham in October 2005. What's it like joining the action so late? Well, if the team is losing the pressure's not really on you, but we were 3–2 up at Craven Cottage and my task was to help keep possession as the clock ran down, so it was unavoidably tense.

At this stage in the procedure, the manager is not going to blind you with science. It'll just be one brisk and simple line, perhaps 'Go and keep the ball' or, in different circumstances, 'Get us a goal'. As a substitute you always have to be ready for any situation, and while people talk blithely about picking up the pace of a game, that's not always easy after you've been warming the bench all afternoon.

Sometimes you jump straight into the flow of the play – Ole Gunnar Solskjaer was the master of that. Every time he went on he was ready to go immediately and he scored a lot of his goals as a sub. But equally, you might find that when you start running at full pace you can't breathe properly for five minutes, even after warming up on the touchline, and then you can find yourself in trouble. On this occasion, everything went according to plan. The score remained the same and we took the points. Job done.

▼ Getting some colourful abuse from Liverpool fans is par for the course when United visit Anfield, but it has never bothered me in the slightest. For one thing, you rarely pick up individual comments because you're concentrating so fiercely on the game, and in the heat of the action you're conscious only of a general background noise. For another, while recognising that Liverpool supporters traditionally despise United, the majority of Merseysiders to me come over as essentially good-tempered. They're classically witty people, the biting humour comes so naturally to them, and even if they were having a go at us I found it very funny listening to them all having a laugh together.

At Liverpool, I think much of the so-called abuse is without malice. I believe they understand good football and can relate to what Manchester United have done over the years. They might say they hate us, but deep down I think there's respect for what we've achieved. It's not been often that I've registered real nastiness at Anfield, certainly not on the scale of the venom we've experienced at Elland Road.

Whatever the attitude of any crowd, Manchester United will never be intimidated by verbal hostility. Wherever we go, it's the other team we think about, not their fans.

◄ I'm having a cough – not a yawn! – at home to West Bromwich Albion on Boxing Day 2005. I get a touch of asthma which can make me very wheezy when the weather gets cold, but it's nothing too serious and I can always sort myself out with a quick puff of my inhaler. I'm covering my hands because I've never been one for wearing gloves during a game, no matter what the temperature. I don't mind using them in training when nobody can see me but not for a match; it would give the wrong impression. After all, football is a winter game. Have I ever been tempted to wear tights? Huh! What do you think?

This was only two days before our game at Birmingham, during which I first experienced the eye problem that was to make me miss half a season. I felt something wasn't quite right in the St Andrews dressing room before kick-off, but I do suffer from migraines and thought I might be getting one of those. But when somebody took a throw in my direction about ten minutes from time I could see three balls coming towards me. It turned out that a blood clot had burst in my left eye and I was told that my sight might not be fully restored. I was always positive I'd get over it, mind, and I did.

► Another season, another goal famine. This header from one of Ryan Giggs' beautifully measured corners skidded into Portsmouth's net one rainy night in December 2005 at a point when I hadn't scored since May. This time it was beginning to seem like I'd never hit the target again and it felt worse than my previous drought because it came at a period when we weren't winning titles – precisely because we were short of goals. I'd been struggling for form, having a really bad time and not getting forward as much as in my younger days, and the contribution to our tally from midfield just wasn't good enough.

Now, at last, my duck was broken and I must admit the slippery conditions at Old Trafford were a real help. I was perhaps ten yards out when I made contact with the ball, which bounced up awkwardly on the wet surface and crept inside an unprotected upright. Maybe the Pompey keeper, Jamie Ashdown, thought he might have been better off with a teammate on the line, but that didn't matter to me. It was just such a huge relief to be up and running as a goalscorer again, and I felt even happier when Ruud van Nistelrooy and Wayne Rooney made it 3–0 shortly before the end.

▼ This is one of the scruffiest goals I've ever scored — and there have been a few! A cross came in from Gary Neville, it bounced in front of me and I just couldn't get my feet sorted out — I didn't know which one to kick it with. In the end I bundled the ball over the line off my shin and turned away for a distinctly sheepish celebration. It seemed a big goal at the time because we had to beat Benfica in their Estadio da Luz to be sure of qualifying for the knockout stage of the 2005/06 Champions League, and this put us in front early on. Sadly for us, we lost 2–1 and said goodbye to Europe in December, five months before we had intended.

Certainly, it was a clumsy finish and, looking back, I have to admit to being embarrassed, but basically I was happy to take any goal, any time. Three seasons later in Milan, I scored an even jammier one, with the ball going in off my standing leg, but they all count. It was an ugly one — so what?

◄ John O'Shea was first on the scene after the ball crept past the bemused Benfica keeper and he was full of questions: 'What on earth was that? What did you put that one in with? How long did you work to perfect that one on the training ground?' Or words to that effect. He thought it was hilarious and had a real belly laugh at my expense.

Sheasy's such a relaxed character – you might call him the archetypal easy-going Irishman – and he was popular with everyone around the club. He's a top-class footballer, too, so versatile that the manager could play him in any position and he'd excel. Despite being right-footed he's had some great spells at left-back, nutmegging people all over the place and doing well at both ends of the pitch. There have been some tremendous stints in central midfield, too, including one particularly effective one alongside Giggsy when we had lots of injuries. He can make goals, he can score goals, he can stop people playing, he's got the lot. He can even go between the posts when we're desperate, as he did once down at Tottenham when he came off his line a treat to take the ball off the toe of Robbie Keane.

Sheasy was at United since he was a kid; he loves the club to bits and it was hard to imagine him not spending the rest of his career at Old Trafford. But then along came Steve Bruce in the summer of 2011 and John joined Sunderland, an apt illustraton of how uncertain life can be in professional football. He's into his thirties now, an old man like me, but I'm sure he's got plenty of years left in him yet. Still, I don't think he'll ever quite work out how I fluked that goal against Benfica . . .

' *I'm laughing at Scholesy here because I'm so used to seeing him score the cleanest of goals, wonder goals really. I'm telling him he's absolutely shanked this one, and that's total shock on my face at seeing him mishit a shot. Mind you, it was a good job he did on this occasion!* '

JOHN O'SHEA

◄ Note the headgear as Wayne Rooney and I limber up for a training session at Carrington with a few stretches. It couldn't have been too cold or I'd have had my head covered, too, so I can only conclude that Wayne was hiding his receding hairline. He does like his hats, and that's got to be the reason why, although that might change after his transplant!

I can joke about Wayne because he loves his banter, and hands out so much of his own. He reminds me a lot of Nicky Butt in that he's lots of fun to be with and he's a great mixer; he's essentially a friendly, down-to-earth character who would do anything for anyone.

Of course, there's no doubt that he has a temper about him, which is sometimes evident on the field. He's a born winner, and if something's upsetting him, then often it shows. Certainly if the team's not playing well or if someone's not doing what they should, then he will make his feelings clear.

Given the way he speaks out and the strength of his character, I can see Wayne as a future Manchester United captain. He has the qualities to drive a side on, to lift his teammates the vital five per cent extra that might be needed to turn a match if things are going badly. I can see similarities to Roy Keane in his determination, his will to win, his prodigious work rate and his readiness to address issues head-on. If Wayne wore the armband with even half as much success and distinction as Roy, then I don't think United fans would be complaining.

❛ Here's Scholesy, probably about to make his latest crack about my bald patch. He could be keeping himself to himself, but then he'd come out with a killer one-liner. So often it was him who put the final nail in somebody's coffin. He's quiet but he speaks his mind, and when he did say something the lads knew he meant it. He was someone younger players could look up to and admire.

For me, Scholesy's the best footballer England has produced in my time. The way he controlled games, passed the ball, saw things that other players didn't see; it was such a pleasure to play with him and United were lucky to have him for so long. ❜

WAYNE ROONEY

12

MOVE OVER, SENHOR MOURINHO

Having just endured three seasons in the title wilderness, we were overjoyed to bring the Premiership crown back to Old Trafford in 2007, and to do it with a little bit to spare. We finished six points clear of Chelsea, who had been going for a hat-trick, and no fewer than twenty-one in front of third-placed Liverpool. Importantly, too, it didn't feel like it was going to be a one-off. We were playing well on an increasingly consistent basis, also reaching the FA Cup final and the last four of the Champions League, which augured well for the future.

It represented an incredible achievement by the manager, who celebrated his twentieth anniversary at the club during the season and had put together a succession of exceptional teams during that time. No matter what star players came and went, Sir Alex Ferguson just kept rolling along, and so did Manchester United. I could hardly believe my own good fortune in being a part of the story for so long.

◄ If ever a professional footballer needs perspective about his own and his family's privileged lifestyle, then I recommend a visit to the Baphumela Home orphanage in Cape Town, South Africa. We called by in July 2006 as part of the club's commitment to UNICEF, and we spent a couple of hours going round to see every child. It is so painfully obvious how much love they need – the whole time we were there they were holding out their arms to be picked up and cuddled – and it's impossible to resist them.

Of course, these children had never heard of Manchester United, we were complete strangers to them, but that didn't matter. We were friendly faces, ready to engage with them and pay them some attention, and that was enough. Having three kids of my own, the plight of these little South Africans really came home to me. I could understand their needs and what they were missing by not having parents.

All the players love doing these visits, although it is heart-rending when we have to wave goodbye. For a long time afterwards I had vivid memories of this little lad, who clung to me as if he was my own. He was so nice and smiley, and all he needed was love.

➤ It's photocall time for myself and Alan Smith, who arrived at Old Trafford like a blast of fresh air from the Yorkshire Moors. The first thing to say about him is that he's a lovely lad, open and honest as the day is long, and when he came to us in the summer of 2004 he was exactly what we needed. We'd had a lot of foreign players in recent times and Alan was a tough, rumbustious centre forward in the grand old English tradition, who brought something refreshingly different to the squad. He had loads of Premiership experience with Leeds and our fans loved the passion and desire he gave to the United cause for every minute he was on the pitch.

Of course, he was, and will always remain, a mad Leeds fan, but as a professional he never had a problem getting over that. He knew that with Manchester United he would be challenging for major trophies every year, and I don't think it would have been too difficult a decision for him to make the switch. With all due respect to Leeds, who had been a top club in the past and have the potential to be so again in the future, it was clear that he had a better chance of collecting medals with us.

Alan turned out to be a terrific signing, doing a tremendous job both up front and in midfield, but he suffered a horrendous injury in an FA Cup tie at Liverpool and was never quite the same player again. At the time of this picture in August 2006, he was preparing for what turned out to be his last season at Old Trafford, during which he battled bravely and played well at times without quite recovering his peak form.

➤ Playing 500 games for one club, especially Manchester United, represents a major milestone which not many people have passed, and I am proud to have done it. What made it even more special was that the person who presented me with a silver plate to mark the achievement, ahead of our Sunday afternoon meeting with Liverpool at Old Trafford in October 2006, was Sir Bobby Charlton.

I'm too young to have seen him play in the flesh, but even so, when I think of United, the first name that springs to mind is Sir Bobby. I've watched film of his goals, so many of them from thirty-five yards and with a heavy leather ball, and I know that he was one of the greatest players ever, a man who always led by example. He remains a massive presence at the club and we all look up to him, learning from him to lead our lives the right way and to try to behave as professionally as he always did.

Not surprisingly, then, I got a little bit emotional when I read his generous remarks about me in his afterword for this book. Honestly, tears were not far away. You don't really know what people think of you until you read something like that, and it left me feeling humble and very grateful.

▲ A fantastic day got even better when we went on to beat Liverpool 2–0 and I managed to score the opening goal. It wasn't pretty but nobody in the United camp was complaining. A cross came in from Ryan Giggs on the left, I had a shot which hit their keeper, Pepe Reina, then the ball bounced up invitingly. Both Sami Hyypia and I lunged for it and I got there first to prod it over the line, with Jamie Carragher behind me, horrified but helpless to intervene. It's always a deep pleasure to score any sort of goal against Liverpool and this was no exception. It came shortly before half-time, and Rio Ferdinand added our second midway through the second period with an absolute screamer into Reina's top corner. Looking back, it's as though I'd been asked to write the script for that whole day – maybe with a little help from Rio!

◀ It might surprise some people to read that most of the United players quite liked Jose Mourinho. True, there was a certain arrogance about him which in another man you would despise, writing him down as a big-headed so-and-so. But somehow the way in which Mourinho made his pronouncements — often outrageous but always shot through with his own brand of supreme confidence — made them acceptable, and sometimes entertaining.

Whatever else is said about him, we always found him gracious after our games with Chelsea, whatever the result. He would always shake the hands of the United players — in this picture I am having a fleeting personal audience with the 'Special One' after our 1–1 draw with Chelsea at Old Trafford in November 2006 — and although there was never time for a proper conversation, I got the impression of a personable guy.

We didn't have happy memories of Mourinho's time before he came to England, just his sprinting down the touchline at Old Trafford after his Porto side had knocked us out of the Champions League. We didn't enjoy that but we could understand his excitement and his record over the seasons that followed speaks for itself.

▼ If technique is the yardstick, this is the best goal I've ever scored — yet listen to our kitman Albert Morgan and he'll tell you that the credit should be his! It happened two days before Christmas 2006 during United's 3–0 victory at Villa Park which kept us at the top of the Premiership table. Ryan Giggs took a left-footed corner from the right, the headed clearance looped high into the night sky and dropped to me, lurking with intent in a central position about twenty-five yards out. Everything seemed just right and, putting modesty to one side, I did volley it perfectly. I didn't try and burst the ball, although it hammered in off the crossbar as though I'd used every last bit of my strength. In fact, that was due far more to timing than power.

What was Albert's part in all this? Well, before the game I'd told him that he'd brought me the wrong boots, my training ones instead of the ones I used for matches. Afterwards he reminded me of my moan and asked me if I wanted to swap back, but I told him not to bother. He did add that he was now a shoe-in for goal of the season!

▲ With the ball safely in the Villa net, I ran off to celebrate with my nearest teammate, Patrice Evra, but I also had a little thought about Albert, and pointed down at my boots. Lucky for him I had got him out of the mire! Just kidding, Albert.

‘ *Paul's a lovely feller but he could be a bit particular about his footwear. Sometimes he'd train in his match boots, sometimes in his training boots, and knowing which ones to put out for him every time could be like juggling soup. On this occasion, he wanted the boots I didn't have, though I knew I had a pair to cover what he needed and I gave them to him. Then he went and scored that wonderful goal, and I'm definitely claiming it for myself. Every time I see it, I say: "That's my goal!"* ’

ALBERT MORGAN

◀ It always pays to listen to someone who knows what they're talking about and that's what I'm doing here. When Henrik Larsson arrived at Old Trafford on loan from the Swedish club Helsingborg in January 2007, he was in his thirty-sixth year, yet on the training pitch and in games he performed like a twenty-one-year-old. Henrik had done great things with top clubs – only recently he had won the Champions League with Barcelona – and he proved to be a fabulous example to everybody at United. His attitude was spot-on, his movement was fantastic and he both scored and created goals. Our forwards, Wayne Rooney in particular, learned so much from him.

Henrik was with us for only ten weeks and everyone at the club wanted him to extend his stay for the rest of the season, but he stuck to his agreement with Helsingborg and we respected him for that, especially as it must have been difficult for him to turn down the chance of chasing more top honours with United.

As a character Henrik was very quiet, but really refreshing to have around the place. He just got on with his work and everything he did was geared to his game on Saturday. He was so quick and sharp and nimble and clever, and it was both a joy and a privilege to play alongside him.

▶ I must admit, delivering a girlie slap to the Liverpool midfielder Xabi Alonso at Anfield in March 2007 and getting sent off for my pains was not my finest hour. In slight mitigation I'd point out that he had been niggling away at me all game, and that when he caught me one more time, my patience snapped and I raised my hand to him, which was stupid of me. I made the most minimal of contact, certainly nothing that was going to hurt him, but it was enough to see the red card and away I trudged to the dressing room, awaiting what seemed like an inevitable bollocking from the manager. I was certain he'd be angry because the score was 0–0 with only four minutes left to play, so I could have cost us the points, but salvation was at hand from an unexpected quarter. Deep inside stoppage time John O'Shea popped up with a winner in front of the Kop and I was off the hook. I owe you one, Sheasy!

As for Alonso, he was a great player for Liverpool and if you saw his name on their teamsheet you knew you were in for a tough challenge. He was well known for his fabulous passing range, something which Liverpool sorely missed when they sold him to Real Madrid, and you knew you had to get close to him or he'd destroy you. He wasn't shy about putting his foot in, either, as any central midfielder has to do, but there was nothing unduly malicious about him and he always had my respect.

United trailed Blackburn 1–0 after an hour on the last day of March 2007, just when our bid to regain the Premiership title should have been gathering pace. Old Trafford was a cauldron of disgruntlement according to the *Match of the Day* commentator, and he was dead right. We weren't playing well, nerves were jangling and, as we hadn't won it for three years on the belt, our fans were understandably anxious.

But then I managed to nick the ball off their big defender Christopher Samba, somehow danced past first Ryan Nelsen and then Stephen Warnock as they came at me (above), which left keeper Brad Friedel still to beat. Having gone so far on a diagonal run from left to right across their box it would have been a crime not to

score, and so I was pretty relieved to hit a low cross-shot into the far corner from about twelve yards (above). Actually I wanted to smash it harder than I did, but I dragged it just a little, which helped it away from Friedel, who always seemed to play a blinder against us.

After that, Blackburn collapsed and we battered them for the last half-hour, winning 4–1 thanks to strikes from Michael Carrick, Ji-Sung Park and Ole Gunnar Solskjaer. Was it the most memorable dribbling goal I ever scored? At the time it was just about the only one, at least since my schooldays, although there was to be another quite similar three years later, which I will come to in due course.

◄ It might have been a coincidence; then again, maybe it wasn't. The day before I amazed myself and, no doubt, everybody else at Old Trafford, by scoring after a dribble against Blackburn, we had this drill in training, zigzagging between the poles to sharpen our movement and make us more nimble. Does that mean coach Micky Phelan is clairvoyant? You can't rule it out!

Ole Gunnar Solskjaer and Alan Smith don't look over-impressed by my efforts; then again, their dour expressions may be entirely due to exhaustion from their last encounter with the poles and dread at contemplating the next. I don't think Alan particularly relished training, though he was no slacker and was always ready for the match. Ole was different, a fantastic worker in training whose input was always top quality, whether at Carrington or in a game. He was a sublime finisher, out of this world, and although he must have missed occasionally, my prevailing image is of him putting away chance after chance after chance.

► It might have been an execution in Rome. Even before the referee brandished the red card above my bowed head, I had that familiar sinking feeling in the pit of my stomach. I had hardly touched Roma's Francesco Totti, but he had gone over screaming, writhing around on the ground, and I knew what the outcome would be. There was nothing wrong with him, he wasn't hurt, but it was a case of 'job done' as far as he was concerned. I was off and we were on our way to a 2–1 defeat in the first leg of our Champions League quarter-final in Italy in April 2007.

I'd already been booked for a foul, and I'd made only two tackles all night. As I've mentioned, it annoyed me so much when I saw some players make five or six tackles before receiving a caution, while whenever I made one the card came out.

I'm crestfallen here because it wasn't even half-time and I knew it was going to be a long night for the rest of the team. I had let them down and I knew I was in for a bollocking from the manager. Pretty well every time I went out he told me to watch my tackling, but he knew I had to make challenges as a central midfielder. Why, there were times when we got beaten and in the dressing room he'd be fuming because, in his words, nobody had even made a tackle!

On this occasion it was 0–0 when I marched, but even though we went on to lose, my dismissal didn't affect the outcome of the tie because we won the return 7–1. I missed that game because of this red card, but it was a pleasure to watch one of the best European performances I've ever seen at Old Trafford.

◄ I suppose you might call this the classic midfield general pose – ball at my feet, just nudging it with the outside of my right boot while looking all around me and contemplating a change in the direction of play. There are few better feelings for a footballer than when your confidence is running high, you feel you're playing well, that what you're doing is working and that you're in control of a game. It's a feeling I'd have liked to experience more often than I did.

As a central midfielder, even before the ball got to me, I'd have had a quick look round and be thinking where it was supposed to go next. People talk about midfielders having a picture of the whole game, and that's exactly what I tried to do, so it was crucial for me to know where everyone was. That was the plan anyway, although unfortunately it didn't always work out like that.

◄ That's a fearsome glower on my face and while I can't explain it for sure – I might be unimpressed with a decision or ruing a bad pass – I can guarantee one thing: that I'm totally immersed in the game. When you're on the pitch your mind has to be right, and if it isn't your teammates and manager can tell. During those ninety-odd minutes, football is all that exists, and any personal matters that are bugging you have to be placed firmly to one side. They simply cannot be allowed to intrude or you will not do your job properly.

Some people have the impression that footballers are not normal human beings with the same problems as everybody else. They don't think we go shopping for food; they believe that someone does everything for us as far as everyday living is concerned. It might be true in a handful of cases, but I can assure you that most of us do our utmost to live as normally as we can.

Of course, there is pressure on us all the time to perform and sometimes that can be difficult for private reasons, yet if players fall below par then they get some stick. I always accepted that totally because that was the nature of the job and I was well paid to do it.

◄ We began our Champions League semi against AC Milan in May 2007 with high hopes of a place in the final, but we had a dreadful night at the San Siro and ended being soundly beaten.

Here, I am evading the out-stretched boot of the combative midfielder, Gennaro Gattuso. He did a brilliant job for them, taking the ball from Cristiano Ronaldo time and time again, and I wouldn't deny that the tough little Italian can be hugely effective, or that he has made a fantastic career out of doing what he does, but when I hear comparisons with Roy Keane it makes me laugh. Certainly he's got limitless desire, he's strong and he's dynamic, but when it comes to all-round technical ability he's not on the same planet as Roy. To me, he's like a cheerleader, getting the fans going and urging on his teammates, admittedly a great quality in itself. Sometimes he can get himself a bit too worked up, though, and the night he clashed with Spurs coach Joe Jordan early in 2011 was clearly one of them.

I've sent Gattuso the wrong way here, but he had the last laugh as our 3–2 first-leg advantage was obliterated by Milan's 3–0 triumph on the night. Twice we suffered horribly in the San Siro at the hands of the Italians before finally getting our own back in 2010.

◄ I'd like to say this shot between Manchester City's Michael Ball and Stephen Ireland on a sunlit Eastlands morning in May 2007 clinched the Premiership title, but I can't because it didn't go in. But no matter, there wasn't long to wait. We won a stormy encounter 1–0, Chelsea dropped two points at Arsenal the next day and we were champions for the first time since 2003.

To all in the United camp, Ball was very much the villain of the piece, terrorising Cristiano Ronaldo and leaving studmarks all over him. I know Cristiano could be a bit theatrical at times, but truly he was targeted mercilessly on this occasion. In the end he made the offender pay in the best possible way by getting up from one

of Ball's foul challenges to score the only goal of the match from the spot. Even then, Ball gave rise to further bad feeling, tumbling dramatically in our area from an innocuous challenge from Wes Brown to win a penalty near the end. Happily, Edwin van der Sar saved Darius Vassell's kick and justice was done.

► Two days can be a long time in football. In the early hours of Thursday morning we had returned from Milan defeated, disappointed and debilitated. Now, as the final whistle sounded at the City of Manchester Stadium, the Premiership crown was as good as ours. We hadn't played brilliantly in the derby but we had dug in and thoroughly deserved the vital three points. My expression is registering both triumph and relief after a tough shift on a hot morning at the end of a tricky week.

➤ I'm usually to be found lurking in the background during presentations, but this time I'm fronting up with a bottle of bubbly when the Premiership trophy was handed over after our final game of the season at Old Trafford. Why the uncharacteristic display of glee? It was because we'd gone three years without winning it, the longest gap of my career, and I was simply overjoyed to get it back. I know it's a shocking waste of champagne, but it looks good in the pictures!

Actually, the game that afternoon against West Ham, which we lost 1–0, was a damp squib from our point of view and I have to admit that our preparation for it might not have been ideal. We'd had a few nights of enjoying ourselves since the title had been put to bed and, although we still expected to win, the meeting with West Ham had not figured prominently in our thoughts. It had been crucial for them, of course, because their victory through a Carlos Tevez goal made certain they wouldn't go down.

▼ Cristiano's telling me I'm unwise to wear the funny spiky hat because it'll mess up my hair, but you won't be shocked to discover that such a risk terrified me rather less than it did him. Here he's immaculately gelled as ever, his barnet miraculously untouched by the goings-on around him.

▲ I was chuffed to bits to receive United's goal of the season award for my effort at Villa Park, and it was so appropriate that the trophy was handed over by a man who knows a thing or two when it comes to scoring goals: Ole Gunnar Solskjaer.

He had just collected his sixth title medal before retiring as a player to concentrate on coaching United's reserves. I am not surprised he did so well at that level and he has now progressed to management with Molde, his former club in Norway. He's a great football man and a smashing person, and I hope he goes on to bigger things further down the line.

➤ I'm boiling at the award of a free kick to Chelsea in the 2007 FA Cup final after I made what I maintain was a perfect tackle on their winger Shaun Wright-Phillips. I got the ball cleanly and sent him spinning up in the air – you can't go much better than that. Obviously there are times when players argue a point even when they know they're in the wrong, hoping to get away with something, but this time I was positive I was in the right.

Losing the 2007 FA Cup final was a miserable note on which to end a memorable season, not least because we played really well. We battered them all game without getting a shred of luck, had a legitimate strike by Ryan Giggs ruled out, then lost to a Didier Drogba finish near the end of extra time.

It was a sad echo of our previous appearance in the final two years earlier, when we had dominated against Arsenal but ended up with nothing to show for our efforts. On both occasions, nobody could have complained if we'd won by two or three goals.

So often we played well against Chelsea but couldn't beat them. They seemed to have a hold over us. They concede possession, not just against us but against a lot of teams, yet they don't let it bother them. They're resilient, they keep going to the end, and certainly during the days of the Mourinho factor, they tended to find a way to win.

▼ A frosty and misty but absolutely beautiful morning at Carrington and I'm waiting for my teammates to leave the dressing room. I was usually the first one out on the training pitch, often marking time while the others fiddled about with their hair gel or whatever. Me, I just came in, put my boots on and went out. I didn't spend too much time in front of the mirror, which is probably obvious when you look at my hairdo.

I think some of the foreign lads take their time getting ready because they don't enjoy our temperatures. I was always hearing from them about how horrendous the Manchester weather was. They moaned about the wind and the rain and the cold, but they were well paid to do their jobs here so I didn't waste too much sympathy on them.

Amazingly to me, our climate can even be a factor in players deciding to leave United. For all we heard about Real Madrid, our average temperature might even have helped Cristiano Ronaldo on his way. I love Manchester as a place, always have and always will, but clearly that affection is not universal. Still, United's footballers are in the best league in the world, getting well paid for their efforts, and they'll have plenty of time to sunbathe when they're older.

13

BLOOD AND PLUNDER
IN THE MOSCOW NIGHT

Somebody wrote that United's Champions League final against Chelsea in Moscow in 2008 represented a shot at redemption for me, because suspension had caused me to miss our astonishing victory over Bayern Munich in Barcelona nine years earlier. In my opinion, that journalist was talking through his hat because I don't think in those terms. To me it was simply a marvellous opportunity to play in the biggest club game in the world and I was determined to make the most of it, especially after being sidelined for three months of the season through injury.

I have to admit that, although we had given some magnificent European performances since that magical night at the Nou Camp in 1999, there was an unavoidable feeling that we had underachieved in the Champions League. After beating Bayern we believed that we could go on a run of success like Real Madrid, AC Milan or Ajax, putting together a sequence of wins that would move us up a level. But year after year we fell in the quarters or semis, which left us desperate to take the next step in 2008.

If ever there was a match in which we wanted to play our best it was the Manchester derby of February 2008, which coincided with the fiftieth anniversary of the Munich air disaster. During the week leading up to the game, the club led deeply moving tributes to the twenty-three people who died in the crash, and we, the modern United, wanted to give an uplifting performance to show our respect on such an important day. Sadly, we just couldn't provide it.

It was poignant and entirely appropriate that we marked the occasion by wearing shirts without the usual sponsorship logos, but our performance on that uniquely emotional afternoon at Old Trafford was horribly disappointing and we lost 2–1.

In the days before the game, there had been a memorial service and blanket media coverage of the anniversary, but instead of the occasion motivating us to put on a fitting display, it somehow got the better of us and we fell woefully flat. Certainly, I had a rotten game; we just couldn't get going and City were well worth their win. In the end it felt like we'd let down a lot of people who had expected a celebration in remembrance of one of the greatest teams there has ever been. Worse still, we felt like we'd let down their memory a little bit. The picture above, taken at the final whistle, sums up the way the day went for us.

◄ What the hell do they want now? Why don't they leave me alone?

Most people know that I've never been a great one for speaking in public. I don't feel comfortable with the notion of people turning up just to listen to what I have to say. I'll admit it's strange, though, that I'm so nervous in front of a microphone when I was totally happy to go out and play in front of seventy-odd thousand people every week. In that situation it was like there was nobody there, I was just doing my job. But in the press room, in front of only twenty or thirty people, it could throw me. Over the years I suppose I got a little bit better with the media, and towards the end of my playing days I wasn't as edgy as I used to be. But, trust me, I'd still avoid it all if I could!

► I'm battling for possession with my former England teammate Steven Gerrard during a typically ferocious clash between United and Liverpool at Old Trafford in March 2008. We won this one 3–0 on our way to the title, which is the prize I believe Liverpool long for each year more than any other. Only once in my career have they gone close to that, when we completed our second hat-trick of Premier League titles in 2008/09, and even then they weren't *that* close.

Given Steven's fabulous talent, he could have gone to virtually any club in the world and picked up all the honours his heart could desire. But just as I'm a typical Manchester boy, so he's Liverpool through and through, and he chose to stay with the team he loves. Credit to him for that.

As a character Steven's quiet. He just gets on with his game, similar to me in many ways. We've never been close, though, not even with England. The rivalry between our clubs saw to that.

▼ You put your left arm in, your left arm out . . . it almost looks like I'm dancing with Nemanja Vidic in training, but one thing is certain – I'd rather be tripping the light fantastic with our rugged Serbian central defender than tackling him! Take it from me, Vida is one very hard lad.

Sometimes you might hear criticism of foreign players who might have plenty of fancy tricks on the ball, but throw them into battle on a freezing wet February night at Bolton, or Stoke, or Blackburn, and they just don't fancy it. Well, Vida does fancy it, no matter how tough the assignment. He relishes the physical challenge of the game, the heading, the tackling, the getting in against fearsome opponents when the chips are down. It took him a little while to settle when he arrived in Manchester, but soon he proved himself to be top quality, not only as a warrior, but also in his use of the ball. Vida is a natural for the role of captain, leading from the front.

▲ The manager, his assistant Carlos Queiroz and Nani are all having a laugh, but I'm glad to see someone's taking training seriously. It looks like I'm trying to tackle all three at once, or maybe I've gone through Sir Alex to get to our Portuguese winger.

Not surprisingly for such a young lad, Nani took time to acclimatise to life and the game in a foreign country, but he's gone on to prove himself an exceptional acquisition. He's a fabulous all-round athlete, so quick and strong; he can score goals, make goals and is brilliant with either foot, which makes him a nightmare to defend against.

He's a nice lad, too, happy to take a joke and well capable of dishing out plenty of stick in his turn. There should be no limit to what Nani can achieve with United over the coming years.

▲ Clearly I'm a yard sharper than these two slowcoaches, Anderson and Louis Saha, who are labouring in my wake during this sprinting session at Carrington. In my dreams. More likely they gave me five yards' start and are about to leave me for dead.

As is evident from his grin here – or might that be a grimace? – Ando is such a happy person; I don't think he's got a care in the world. He's great to have around the place because invariably he lightens the mood, just like Dwight Yorke did in his time. Ando has all it takes to be a tip-top performer, too. There have been sequences of games when he's been spellbinding, so quick and aggressive that he's on opponents before they realise. He needs to score more goals, and it's fair to say that sometimes he gets his passing going really well, while at other times it can desert him. I believe that when he gets a bit older, perhaps a little more concentrated, Ando will be awesome.

As for Louis, when he is on song and fully fit there is no better centre forward in the world. It's just a shame that his career has been so cruelly blighted with injuries.

► With another Premier League title on the horizon, we went to Blackburn looking for a win in April 2008, but with only two minutes left we were a goal down. Then Nani delivered a right-footed corner from the left, I arrived in the box and did my damnedest to head the equaliser. But the ball glanced off my forehead and Carlos Tevez, reading the situation in a split second, somehow twisted his body to nod in at the back post. Occasionally a misdirected attempt on goal can be as effective as the most perfectly executed effort, and this was one of those times. I couldn't try to kid anyone that I'd deliberately directed the ball to Carlos, that would be stretching credulity too far. I was definitely aiming for the net and the ball was going two or three yards wide until he stepped in.

The fact that I'm only 5ft 7in could be an advantage for me because opponents didn't really expect me to win headers. I know I've managed to score with a few, but people still thought they didn't have to be so careful about picking me up. But, as I've said, if you meet the ball right, it doesn't matter how tall you are. Ironically, Carlos is one of the few players who's even smaller than me and he did a brilliant job for United. It was a big moment in the title race because although the game ended in a draw, it felt like a win to us, and our morale was sky-high as we faced the home straight.

▲ I'm winning the ball and my opponent is sailing through the air – now that's an image I can really relish! This forceful coming-together with the Wigan midfielder Wilson Palacios happened at the JJB Stadium (now the DW) as we won the 2007/08 Premier League title on the last day of the League campaign. The way he's flying is a typical South American reaction, it's the way they're brought up, but as long as I end up in possession it suits me fine to leave them to their acrobatics.

Palacios, who went on to play for Spurs, was one of Steve Bruce's marvellous buys during his time at Wigan, and the lad did really well for the club alongside his fellow Ecuadorian Antonio Valencia, who has since joined United. Very few people in England had heard of them when they arrived but they soon showed their quality and proved that bargains can still be found.

Here's a couple of contrasting takes of me in celebration mode after Ryan Giggs had secured a 2–0 victory over Wigan – and with it the championship – with his beautifully calm finish at the JJB.

◄ Not for the first time, it looks like I'm wishing the camera was pointing in another direction, but I'm not really glum, rather I'm feeling relieved. A lot of emotion goes into a long chase for the title, especially when it all comes down to the final game, and I'm just having a quiet moment, glad that it's all over. Also I'm looking out for my son, Arron, who was coming down from the stand to join in the lap of honour.

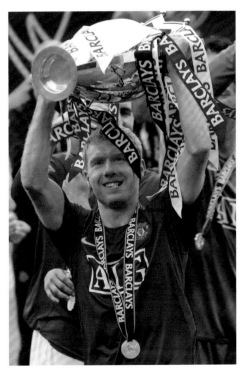

◄ The expression is happier here, even if it looks a bit like I'm grinning through gritted teeth. It's always special to win the title on the pitch, rather than through the results of someone else when we're not playing, though obviously we're delighted to take it however it comes. Certainly I'd rather it was in our own hands instead of sitting at home with my nerves twanging, probably jumping up and down from my seat like a yo-yo, not knowing what to do next. At least if you just have to win your own game, you've got some measure of control over your destiny.

Tangling with two of the most gifted football artists on the planet, Lionel Messi (above) and Andres Iniesta (opposite), at Barcelona's Nou Camp in the first leg of the Champions League semi-final in April 2008. We got a goalless draw that night, though in all honesty we were second best creatively; we didn't play any football that was remotely in their league. But defensively we were fantastic and that got us through.

Facing Barcelona is the ultimate test because they are the best team in the world. Afterwards you need a week to recover because your concentration has to be all-consuming, and therefore it's utterly exhausting. Barca play the sort of football I aspire to, the sort that anybody who plays the game, and really knows the game, would like to emulate. When you merely watch them, and don't have to worry about stopping them, they take your breath away. They give meaning to the phrase

'total football' because the goalkeeper, the centre half, everybody, they can all play beautifully, and they all work their socks off, even the stars.

I am not close to them, but it's easy to tell that the Barcelona lads are fundamentally modest people. There is no hint of conceit about them; they are relaxed about what they do, and they express themselves and their sheer enjoyment of life by the way they play their football. That has been instilled into them by their manager, Pep Guardiola, who adopted the same style in his playing days.

Until recently, Iniesta and his midfield partner Xavi have been relatively unsung compared to, say, Messi, but people inside the game have been raving about them both for years. As for Messi himself, he scores forty or fifty goals a season and he's just awesome. He plays football from the playground and the streets, but in a professional way, and he's a joy to behold.

This is by far the most important goal I've ever scored – the winner against Barcelona at Old Trafford in the second leg of our Champions League semi-final in April 2008 – and it came courtesy of a miskick! Well, maybe I shouldn't be too hard on myself in the circumstances . . . let's call it a *slight* miskick.

It happened like this: Cristiano Ronaldo was dispossessed on the edge of their area and the loose ball bounced out to me, perhaps twenty-five yards from goal. It sat up nicely for a half-volley and, with Lionel Messi looking on but too far away to intervene, I shot in the general direction of goal. There was no cunning plan, all I was trying to do was hit the rectangle, and this is where I was a little bit lucky. The ball sliced ever so slightly off the outside of my right foot, which took it away from keeper Victor Valdes into the top corner of his net (below). In an ideal world I would have started the ball outside his opposite post so that it faded back inside it. Of course, if I'd done that, if I'd made perfect contact, it might easily have come back too much and ended up in Valdes' arms.

As it was – and here I have to resort to a cliché – I was certain it was going in from the moment I hit it. There was a huge gap to the keeper's left – he's not the biggest – and there was no way he was going to reach it. People who play the game every day would have known it wasn't the cleanest of strikes, despite all the praise that was flying about. I was well aware that in terms of execution it didn't come up to the previous season's strike at Villa, but it was more memorable because it was the only goal of the semi-final and it took us to Moscow. That said, Edwin, Rio, Nemanja and company had to defend for their lives over the course of 180 minutes, so it was very much a team effort.

Come to Rio! Our centre half is definitely the one to get the celebrations going when we score a goal, and I'd hazard a guess that he was particularly pleased to go in front against Barcelona. We're all looking reasonably happy with life, aren't we? How could we not be, with United on the way to our first Champions League final for nine years? I never had the feeling that I had to score a goal to get us to Moscow because I'd missed out on our previous final, but I can't deny this was a special moment. Ji-Sung Park (above) and Michael Carrick (opposite) thought so, too.

❛ *This was a truly fabulous goal, but nothing more than we had come to expect from Scholesy. I could never get bored talking about him, he was my favourite player. I loved watching him because he did everything you'd want to see in a footballer. He could dictate the pace of a game; he could take it by the scruff of the neck and control it; he could score decisive goals; he could make the killer pass; he could switch the play, open teams up, slow the game down, quicken it up; whatever was needed. He would take the ball anywhere on the pitch, which was a big thing for teammates. His best attribute was his tackling – hang on, better scrub that bit! – though actually he was such a clever reader of the game that often he didn't need to tackle anyway.*

He was such a selfless footballer, too, never doing anything for personal glorification, always working for the team. He was never going to change from the sound outlook he had as a kid. Scholesy was the man, all right. ❜

RIO FERDINAND

▼ The completely accidental coming-together with Chelsea midfielder Claude Makelele during the Champions League final in Moscow left me with a bloody nose, a yellow card and a sharp sense of injustice.

The ball bounced between us, both of us were determined to win it and both of us led with our arms, as you have to do sometimes to keep your balance. We collided and I don't know what part of his anatomy connected with my nose, but it was very hard and certainly I came off worst. For some reason their players were in a bit of an uproar about it, thinking I had tried to elbow Makelele, but nothing could be further from the truth. I can only guess that the impact made the challenge look worse than it was. All I know is that there was no way I was attempting to hurt him, and I couldn't understand for the life of me why I was booked.

▼ The messy aftermath of my clash with Makelele, who had walked away with no apparent damage — and no yellow card to match mine! The gore is pouring from my nose, which hurt a lot and which just wouldn't stop bleeding at first. I had to leave the pitch and the doctor manipulated my hooter, seeming to click it back into place while the red stuff was splashing everywhere, which wasn't pleasant. I managed to go back on and I'm happy to say that soon afterwards I played a part in the move that led to Cristiano Ronaldo's fantastic header, which put us in front.

Meanwhile, Makelele didn't seem affected at all, continuing to be as influential as ever in his holding role in front of their defence. There was nothing flashy about him, he didn't score goals or make long passes, but he was a terrific all-round footballer who did so much of the donkey work for his team, winning the ball and giving it to the men in front of him. Previously he had done the same job for Real Madrid and it was significant that when he was gone, despite all their superstars, they missed him badly.

▼ It's not like me to play up to the photographers by kissing my medal, but this time I was that happy I'd have done virtually anything they'd asked me. Did my mind flash back to 1999, when I missed the Champions League final through suspension? Of course it did. I was handed a medal in Barcelona, but it didn't really count for me because I didn't play in the game. This time I'd been on the pitch and made a contribution. This was the real thing. I think my performance was an average one, not bad but not brilliant, though certainly I was part of the team that deserved to lift the trophy. Ryan Giggs replaced me near the end of normal time, and I had no complaints about that. You'd always rather stay on, but I was tiring a little bit and my head was still fuzzy from being swiped on the nose. The manager made the right decision, as usual.

In the first half we had a few chances to put the game beyond Chelsea, but as usual against these opponents we didn't take enough of them and they made us pay with an equaliser before half-time. After that they went very close to beating us, but the result was a fair one and it went to a penalty shoot-out.

As a fellow pro I did have a little bit of sympathy for John Terry, who missed the crucial spot-kick for them. I'd suffered the same thing against Arsenal in the FA Cup final, so I know how demoralising it can be. At the end he was crying, and I just tapped him on the shoulder. I didn't say anything because no words can make you feel any better.

▲ You might say I got a bit carried away at the final whistle, thanks to Wayne Rooney. He swept me right off my feet, and by the state of my splattered nose, it looks as if he might have kidnapped me and beaten me up first! Certainly, he's hoisted me on to his shoulder as if I was weightless. Now, I know I'm the team midget, but Wayne's that strong he could do the same to anybody at Old Trafford, which is why I always try to stay in his good books.

> *We'd just won the Champions League and at times like that there's so much euphoria in the air that you hardly know what you're doing. Good job I didn't drop him!*

WAYNE ROONEY

▲ If an alien craft had happened to be passing over the Luzhniki Stadium, Moscow, after Manchester United had taken possession of the European Cup, then the spacemen inside it would have thought we were a very strange species indeed. As the rain teemed down and midnight approached, there we were gathered in

the middle of a soggy field, engulfed in spiralling tinsel and the swirling smoke of fireworks, all the while bouncing up and down and singing at the tops of our voices. In fact, the real party was yet to begin, and as the night wore on there might even have been a few of those aliens joining in . . .

Winning the Champions League is the ultimate achievement for any club footballer, and it was wonderful to be able to share the joy with my family. At least, it was fabulous that my wife, Claire, and our two oldest children – Arron, who was nine, and Alicia, eight – were able to be in Moscow on that magical night, my only sadness being that our little one, Aiden, was a bit young to travel.

I knew where they had been sitting, about twenty rows back from the dugout, and much as I wanted to bring them down at the end, I hesitated at first because I thought it might seem a bit daft. But then I saw Edwin van der Sar's boy on the pitch, so I signalled for my two to join me and I'm so glad I did because it was such an incredible experience for them.

Arron absolutely adores United, he's a real fanatic who goes to lots of the games and can tell you everything about the club. Claire told me he was singing and chanting throughout the whole 120 minutes against Chelsea. He loves all the songs and the banter; he was totally involved and enchanted by the whole thing. Probably because I've picked him up (above), he's looking a bit embarrassed – I guess he takes after his dad when it comes to being the centre of attention – but actually he was having the time of his life.

Alicia is a big United fan as well. She had a great night, too, and in years to come they'll both love looking back at these pictures with the European Cup. As for Claire, she stayed in the stand. Generally speaking, wives don't run on to the pitch – that might be a little *too* embarrassing!

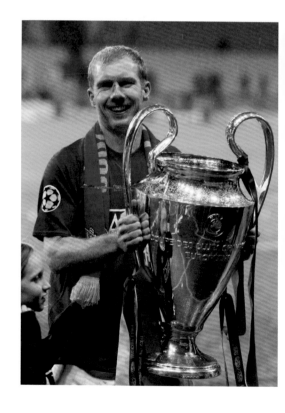

◄ Here's a rare sight — me wearing the captain's armband. It was in a pre-season friendly against Urawa Red Diamonds in Saitama, Japan, during our summer tour in 2007 and I was only filling in because the obvious candidates were not on the pitch.

The fact is that I'm not cut out to be a skipper. I've never been a captain sort of person, not at school or any level since then. Some people are born leaders and you know from the age of six or seven that they will be captains one day. Bryan Robson, Steve Bruce, Roy Keane, Gary Neville, they all come into that category, but I've never been comfortable with the role. You have to be vocal to be a leader and I'm quiet by nature. I'd rather be out of the way, out of the limelight. I don't want to be the commanding officer; I'd rather just be one of the soldiers.

I think the manager realised that at the end of my career and if the usual choices were missing he tended to give the job to another of the lads who had been around a long time. I was happy with that — you might say I was relieved!

14

2008/09

A DOUBLE HAT-TRICK AND A SHARP LESSON

It's easy to look at the 2008/09 campaign and mope because we finished it on such a low note, being outclassed by Pep Guardiola's scintillating Barcelona side on a crushingly disappointing night in Rome. But while it would be wrong to brush our Champions League final horror under the carpet – and there isn't a club in the world that doesn't have so much to learn from the likes of Messi, Xavi, Iniesta and the rest – United could point to another fabulously successful domestic season.

Becoming the first club ever to complete a second hat-trick of League titles, despite being challenged by a rival in Chelsea whose spending power was infinitely more extensive than our own, was a fabulous achievement and certainly I see my involvement in it as one of the highlights of my career. It was satisfying, too, for me to pick up my first League Cup winner's medal, even if our display in the final against Tottenham at Wembley left plenty to be desired.

▼ Meeting football-crazy youngsters anywhere in the world is uplifting, which is why I enjoyed coaching these twelve and thirteen-year-olds from the Township Soccer League in Cape Town when United visited South Africa in the summer of 2008. There were a few exercises, a little ball-work, some chat and finally a question-and-answer session, which revealed remarkable enthusiasm for the game and an amazing knowledge of Manchester United.

I was delighted by the high level of skill among these boys and girls, who had plainly dedicated a lot of time and effort to their game, which reinforces the view that there is no better way of keeping kids off the streets.

In this case they had good facilities in what seemed to be a decent area, but that is not always the case. Sometimes, on our travels, we encountered people living in abject poverty. I found that extremely distressing, given all the advantages our own children enjoy, but also it was inspiring to see how they just got on with their lives. Most astonishing of all, wherever we went, no matter how low the living standards might have been, we met people with a sunny outlook, singing and dancing and smiling all the time. That certainly taught us a lesson or two about our own perspectives.

► That arm round my shoulder is hugely symbolic because Sir Alex Ferguson has always been a father figure to me and to the rest of the lads who have come through the ranks at Old Trafford. We have all learned so much from him down the years. Even the football gospel preached to us by Brian Kidd and Eric Harrison when we were boys came from the manager originally. If you've got any problem, on or off the pitch, Sir Alex is the person to go and see. He's really sympathetic if there are family issues and he'll always give you time to sort them out.

Obviously the relationship has developed over the years. When I first knew him I was a little boy of around twelve and now, a quarter of a century later, I'm thirty-six. So what's changed? Well, probably I'm not quite so scared of him now! Don't get me wrong, there's still an element of fear, but back in my schooldays it could be a terrifying experience to see him coming down the corridor towards you. Given his reputation, he was someone I definitely tried to avoid!

But then you grow up and you understand why he does what he does. Occasionally he'll ask the opinion of the senior players, though not too often. Usually it will be to do with the mood of the camp, perhaps if we've had some bad results. Of course, even when he's heard what we have to say he will do what he wants.

One of the manager's strengths is getting the best out of people. We have such a big squad these days and if a player's been training all week then he'll believe that he's got a chance of making the team on Saturday. Simple mathematics will tell you that not everybody can be there; not everybody can even get a place on the bench. In those circumstances it can't be easy to keep us all motivated, but the manager has a way of doing it, and that's a part of his greatness.

▲ Football can be a grimly serious business sometimes but here's one of those increasingly rare light-hearted moments. I'm helping Bolton midfielder Kevin Nolan to his feet and we both find the situation funny, although his grin does seem a little more rueful than mine. What's happened? Probably I took him out with a tackle, but we both know he's not hurt so there's no problem.

I don't know Kevin personally, I only ever see him on the football pitch, but he's a fine player and a fair opponent so I do welcome this sort of good-humoured encounter. No matter what anyone thinks, I'm not someone who gets that angry with opposition players and I regret that a lot of the enjoyment has gone from the game because there is so much at stake financially these days. Everyone has become so professional and regimented that we're almost like robots out there running around on the grass. There's not much flair; there aren't many players in the game today who just go out to have some fun. And that's a pity.

▶ It's a snowy day at Carrington and I'm preparing my next bomb for some unlucky victim, who is about to get it on the back of the head. Not the manager, absolutely not, I wouldn't dare! From the look on my face it's more likely to be the photographer.

▼ Cristiano Ronaldo is one of the best footballers I've ever seen, and images of his glorious exploits for United will never leave me. But this is how I'll always remember him, too – as a happy-go-lucky workmate, a congenital joker who loved to take the mick at every opportunity. Here he's obviously not getting at my headgear, of which I'm sure he was jealous, but is having a go at one of the other lads, probably about what they're wearing.

The thing most people don't realise about Cristiano is his professionalism. There was no element of fluke about what he did for us, and is now doing for Real Madrid. We know he had the God-given talent, but also he had a top-class attitude to every aspect of his work, putting in the hard yards every day. He was always practising. Of course, he was a magnificent athlete, too, a tough lad who took loads of physical punishment but always bounced back for more, and who was ultra-confident, both on and off the pitch.

Because Cristiano was handsome, young, carefree-looking, a lot of people thought he was a bit of a playboy during his time in Manchester, but nothing could have been further from the truth. He never lived the high life, he was totally dedicated to his job, and he reaped the rewards.

He worked hard on his English, too, which always helps foreign players to settle. It wasn't great at first, but he tried to speak in English all the time. I guess talking to me must have improved his grammar and vocabulary no end!

▲ Sometimes you can hit a shot perfectly, exactly as you intended, and it goes straight to the goalkeeper. Then again, you can score with a scratchy little bobbler, which is exactly what happened here in our 2–1 FA Cup win over Spurs at Old Trafford in January 2009.

It was an effort directly from a corner, but not in the style of the one at Bradford which people keep reminding me about. The ball came to me along the ground; I concentrated on keeping my shot low despite Michael Dawson's attempted block, and I've dragged it a little bit. Luckily it took a deflection off Tom Huddlestone before creeping into an unguarded corner of the net.

It was my first goal of the season, a welcome end to my latest famine – the drop in my strike-rate is a telling indication that I've settled into more of a sitting midfield role as I've grown older – but more importantly it equalised an early effort by Roman Pavlyuchenko. We had been struggling to this point, but Dimitar Berbatov added a second only a minute after I had scored and we won 2–1.

▲ Here is the closest I've ever got to replicating my goal from David Beckham's corner at Bradford in 2000. This effort was at Old Trafford against Fulham in February 2009, with Michael Carrick supplying the ammunition. I volleyed it crisply enough, but if I'm honest I'd have to say that their keeper, Mark Schwarzer, might be disappointed he didn't make the save. Admittedly, he probably saw it late as it came through a ruck of bodies, but he got quite a strong hand to it and it only just spun over the line.

It was the first time since Bradford that I've managed a goal like this – I don't count the one against Spurs in the FA Cup, because that was a scuff – not least because a lot of teams started marking me just outside the box when they conceded a corner. I've made a few decent connections, but nothing as sweet as the volley at Valley Parade. This one came at a more telling point in the game, though, starting us off on a 3–0 victory, whereas we were already in a strong position at Bradford.

▼ I've been seen as an elder statesman for some time now, but passing is one skill that age doesn't completely wither, as I'm attempting to demonstrate here by chipping the ball in to a forward who is getting behind his defender in my 600th game for United, at home to Portsmouth in April 2009.

People did associate me with starting attacks by knocking long balls and I spent time practising the skill, which looks fine when it comes off but can make you look stupid if it goes wrong. In training I worked with a coach, hitting maybe half a dozen deliveries to either wing. I'd have done more but I needed to save my energy for the games. You lose a bit of strength in your legs as you get older, but the essential technique remains so I was able to pass well as long as I could play. The accuracy came through plenty of practice and having the luck to be born with the necessary technique.

The crowd seemed to enjoy it and so did I. I suppose it became something of a trademark over the last few years when I wasn't scoring so many goals. Certainly it was satisfying to be the starting point of attacks and I was always fortunate to have such excellent wingers and fullbacks to find with my passes. They all knew that if I got on the ball and I didn't see the centre forward with a chance to go through on goal, then I'd be looking for them. For instance, as soon as I received the ball on the left, I always knew that Gary Neville would be haring down the right touchline. We could rely on each other, which is exactly what being part of a team is all about.

▼ Every picture tells a story, and this one had a dismal ending for Manchester United. It was the spring day in 2009 when we lost 4–1 at home to Liverpool, and here the contrast between the body language and facial expressions of Fabio Aurelio and myself could hardly be more stark. He was on cloud nine after curling in a free kick at the Stretford End to make it 3–1 immediately after the sending-off of Nemanja Vidic, while I was grumpily contemplating the inevitability of an unthinkable defeat at the hands of our fierce rivals. I'd only been on the pitch for three minutes, called from the bench to replace Anderson about a quarter of an hour from the end. At that point there had been genuine hope of a comeback, but I didn't do much to improve matters.

Oddly enough, we had gone in front and I didn't think we played too badly. They just took their chances on the day; games can pan out like that. All we could do was hold our hands up, admit we were well beaten and move on to the next match against Fulham. Unsettlingly, we lost that, too, but it was only a battle and not the whole war . . .

▲ If I'm going to be scrupulously truthful, there is almost as much relief as joy in this United celebration at the climax of the League Cup final penalty shoot-out against Spurs at Wembley in March 2009. Anderson had just stroked home beautifully from the spot to clinch the trophy, but actually we were very lucky to get the goalless draw which took it to this stage. Spurs controlled much of the game and their right-winger, Aaron Lennon, gave Patrice Evra problems all afternoon. They made chance after chance and it's no coincidence that the man of the match was our keeper, Ben Foster.

Strangely, perhaps, it's Ryan and me — the old fellers — who are leading the cheers, waving our fists the highest. Mind, if Anderson had been standing in line with us it's a fair bet that he would have been the most prominent. That boy does love a knees-up. As it was, we were delighted with his penalty technique, just as we had been in the Champions League final against Chelsea. I didn't take one on either day — the manager had more sense!

◄ This was a magical moment for me, something really special. I loved getting the kids on the pitch when United had won something and my only disappointment when we became European champions in Moscow was that Aiden, my youngest, wasn't able to be there. But when we drew at home to Arsenal to win the Premier League title on the penultimate day of the 2008/09 season, I had all three children with me.

It was amazing for Arron, Alicia and Aiden to walk out at Old Trafford in front of more than 76,000 people, and to be photographed with that big, lovely trophy. I suppose they didn't realise it at the time, being kids, but when they look back in years to come they'll understand how lucky they were to have had the experience.

The celebrations came as a blessed relief at the end of a tense afternoon which I had spent entirely on the bench. We needed only a point to be certain of the title, but Arsenal kept us sweating all the way to the final whistle, with Cesc Fabregas rattling the post five minutes from the end and Robin van Persie sending a free kick narrowly wide right at the death. But the game finished goalless, and after that it was all enjoyment.

◄ It was the eighth time for Gary, the ninth for me and the *eleventh* for Ryan, but lifting the Premier League trophy was something none of us ever tired of doing. Gary retired in February 2011, but I was delighted that the last two old fellers standing from the early 1990s could join him in a corner of the Old Trafford dressing room to brandish this very special piece of silverware.

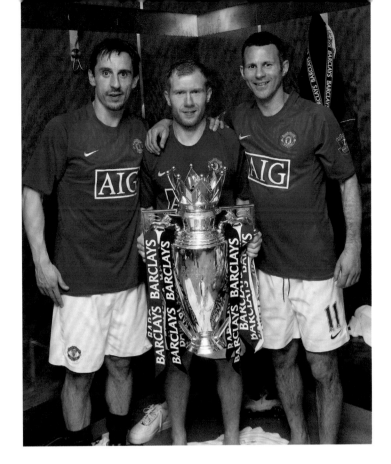

Three old soldiers with the spoils of victory. Every time we won a trophy it was the best night of our lives. We were home-grown lads, playing for the club we loved, experiencing the good and the bad together, the defeats just as much as the wins. We grew to be so close, just like brothers, both on and off the pitch. You go through the personal things, you have children, you have problems, things that life throws at you; you know each other inside out.

I sat next to Paul in the dressing room for fifteen years; I'd go round to his room when we were in a hotel, particularly in the last few years after Philip and David left; I was next to him on most of the flights. He's a terrific person to be in company with, to have a drink with, he's always funny in his dry way. He's a very private individual, though, talking only to those people he trusts, the type of guy who would tell you on the Monday that his wedding is on the following Sunday. "I've got a do on Sunday, do you fancy coming? I'm getting married." That's typical Scholesy – no grand build-up to anything, always matter-of-fact, just getting on with life. An absolutely brilliant man.

GARY NEVILLE

▲ It's no fun losing a Champions League final, even when the opponent jumping for joy a few yards away from you when the final whistle sounds is the majestic player that is Xavi. For my money he's the top midfielder in the world at the minute, and the only man who gets anywhere near him is his teammate, Andres Iniesta. That's why I took it as a supreme compliment when I heard that Xavi had some nice things to say about me and the way I play the game.

Without being the slightest bit flashy, Xavi and Iniesta are the ones who make their team tick, and that's the ultimate job of a midfielder. To watch their football, the sublime passing and the fluid movement, is an absolute joy — at least it is when you're not playing against them, as we were in the 2009 final in Rome's Olympic Stadium.

▼ The expressions on the faces of Ryan Giggs and myself say it all as we wait to receive our losers' medals. There is no point in dressing it up; we had to hold our hands up and admit that we had just lost the most important match in club football to a superior team. It was going through both our minds that Barcelona had been on a different footballing planet to Manchester United that night in Rome and, given that our expectations had been so high, we're totally gutted, especially as we didn't play anything near as well as we can.

Mingling with the inevitable disappointment, though, was an enormous slice of admiration for a truly brilliant team. We felt no animosity towards them; they had played us off the park and they got exactly what they deserved. I had spent most of the evening on the bench, only joining the action after seventy-five minutes when we were two down, by which time, barring a miracle, our fate had been decided.

However, having accorded Barcelona their due, I have to stress that they *are* beatable. There'll be a lot of teams who face them knowing they have no chance and just accepting the situation. But we're not one of those. The trick is to play your own game, not theirs, because you're never going to pass them off the park. You've got to understand that you'll concede possession for long periods, you've got to defend intelligently and hope you can nick something at the other end. Still, it should be the ambition of every other major club to reach the performance level Barcelona show week in and week out. They must be the benchmark for all of us.

◄ The light of battle is in the manager's eye, and that eye is glued to the ball in fierce concentration – don't be misled by the grin – as he takes me on at a game of two-touch in training ahead of the 2009 Champions League final against Barcelona in Rome.

A few years ago he used to join in quite a bit, often by playing in our boxes exercise, which involves two lads in an eight-yard square attempting to get the ball while perhaps eight other players around the outside do their damnedest to keep it away from them. It's all one-touch stuff and the rules are that if one of the outsiders gives the ball away then he's got to go into the box.

The trouble was, the manager always refused to go in, always made out it was somebody else's fault if the ball was lost. To be fair, you could see he had a nice left foot, and he always loved taking penalties. Nobody could ever save them – or perhaps I should say nobody dared to save them!

As for our game here, he would definitely have wanted to win – and probably I let him. No, come to think of it, I must have beaten him because I ended up on the bench against Barcelona . . .

 ❛ *Why else would I put him on the bench against Barcelona? Little upstart! How dare he embarrass his boss? Actually, this takes me back to my halcyon days when I could manage a jog of sorts. I used to love the boxes all right, but Scholesy's wrong in one respect. The players never allowed me to go in the middle in case I showed them up!* ❜

SIR ALEX FERGUSON

15

2009/10

A PECK ON THE CHEEK WOULD HAVE BEEN FINE . . .

It seems that for an awful lot of people, the defining image of United's 2009/10 season was of Gary Neville getting so carried away by his joy at my late winner in the springtime derby against City, which kept our hopes of a fourth successive title flickering, that he grabbed me for, shall we say, a tender moment of celebration. I'm sure readers will empathise when I say that, from a personal perspective, the shot of me actually heading the goal evokes a rather more pleasant memory!

In the end, unfortunately, we were unable to catch Chelsea, finishing just a point adrift and thus missing out on what would have been a unique achievement. Still, having bidden farewell to the world-class talents of Cristiano Ronaldo and Carlos Tevez during the previous summer, I'd say we gave a pretty decent account of ourselves. Wayne Rooney played the best football of his life to date – although I'd be surprised if there isn't even better to come from him – and a new wave of youngsters made encouraging strides. As for me, the old joints were beginning to creak ominously . . .

◄ I love a day at the races, especially with such a reliable body of tipsters as I'm with here at Kempton Park in September 2009. After we won the Champions League a group of us bought a horse called Moscow Eight, which turned out to be a bit of a disappointment, invariably finishing well down the field as it did on this occasion. In fact, I wouldn't be surprised if it's still running!

Now we've got a string of new horses which we keep with Michael Owen's trainer, and we're relying on Michael to live up to his reputation as an expert. He's the one we look to for advice and here, as pretty well always when he's not on the football pitch, he's clutching the *Racing Post*, which he calls his bible.

John O'Shea, on the right, is our Irish specialist. He's got contacts over the water and he gets us lots of good information, although it doesn't seem to make any difference. Here we're weighing up the prospects along with Michael Carrick (left) and Jonny Evans (behind Sheasy), two more members of our syndicate.

Racing is a relaxing way to spend some time away from football and I like taking the kids when I get the chance. In an ideal world I'd get along to a meeting every couple of weeks, but when I was playing I was lucky if I made it half a dozen times a year. The horses usually made for a hot topic of conversation with the manager, who tended to give us the odd bad tip here and there . . .

' *The Red Army partnership, as we call ourselves, have a few horses – Cuban Peace, Cuban Spirit and Cuban Quality – which we keep at Michael Owen's yard, and Paul's a keen part of the set-up. He's very knowledgeable, with a couple of friends who study the form, and he's quite canny. He doesn't give out tips very often, but when he does they're usually worth following.*

You need a sense of humour to follow racing. We're not big winners, but we get a lot of enjoyment from the occasional day out, like this one at Kempton Park. I can't recall what horse we had running that day, only that it didn't win. '

JOHN O'SHEA

▼ Sunshine lights up a woodland glade, there's a smile on my face and a football in the air — have I died and gone to heaven? Not exactly. This is Carrington, United's training ground, where we certainly get our share of traditional Manchester weather and where we generate an enormous amount of sweat. That said, you'll never hear me grumble about my place of work.

Carrington is only ten minutes out of Manchester and has all the state-of-the-art facilities needed by a modern club, yet we're in the countryside, with open fields all around and horses just down the road. Apart from the very occasional eruption by someone I don't need to name, it's always been a truly peaceful environment and United's players are very lucky to have it.

▲ I scored the first of my two goals against Manchester City in the 2009/10 campaign during the second leg of the League Cup semi-final at Old Trafford, putting us level on aggregate after we had lost 2–1 at Eastlands. The ball was laid to me inside the box by Michael Carrick and I just managed to reach it before Pablo Zabaleta. I got my shot away, the ball squirmed under his foot and it didn't give keeper Shay Given a lot of chance to stop it on its way into the bottom corner. We went 2–0 up through Michael, then Carlos Tevez pulled one back for City before Wayne Rooney settled it at the death. That was one of three late winners we scored against City that term, which must have been totally debilitating for them. Lovely!

◀ My glee at nailing our equaliser against City is about to be shared by my fellow midfielder Darren Fletcher, who has been one of United's best and most consistent performers in recent times. He got a lot of stick early in his career, but he's a strong character and he came through it, coping with the criticism really well and always persevering. He's usually especially effective in the games against our main rivals, which is a useful attribute to have, and he richly deserved the new long-term contract he was handed in 2011.

Darren's a smashing lad, too. He used to be very quiet when he was younger, but now he's come out of his shell and is as quick to take the mick as anyone. For the record, I wasn't in the team for the final at Wembley in which the lads beat Aston Villa to retain the trophy.

Paul Scholes set the perfect example for any youngster coming into professional football. He didn't promote himself; he wasn't interested in interviews and suchlike; he was happy to go unnoticed. As a result, for a long time it was only people with an exceptionally keen eye for the game who realised exactly how great a player he was. In fact, mostly we're talking about people who played with and against him, because that was when you truly appreciated his talent. Therefore it didn't surprise me in recent years when so many of the world's top performers queued up to pay him the handsome compliments he so richly deserved.

To discover the only reason why he didn't pick up any of the top individual awards, we come back to the fact that he was never a self-publicist. But if you study his record, and picture what he was like on the pitch, the inescapable conclusion is that he should have been up there repeatedly when the votes were counted for European and World Footballer of the Year. I have so much respect for his achievements, and also for the genuinely humble person that he has always remained. Scholesy is a man to look up to in every conceivable way.

DARREN FLETCHER

▲ It was the worst, the flukiest, the most downright comical goal I ever scored in my life. During the Champions League clash with AC Milan at the San Siro in February 2010, Darren Fletcher crossed from the right and as it reached me I tried to hit the ball with my right foot. I might have got a tiny bit of contact on it, but nowhere near enough to send it towards goal. Instead it hit my left shin and squirted away, totally out of control, before trickling into the net at the far post.

Of course, Alessandro Nesta and his fellow defenders couldn't be expected to read a situation like that and the poor old keeper, Dida, had no chance. You might call it embarrassing, but in a massive game against Milan, honestly, you don't care how they go in. All you can do is think back to those endless hours on the training pitch perfecting the manoeuvre, making sure your shinpad is in exactly the right place for the ball to bounce off . . .

▼ What's Ronaldinho saying here? Arise Sir Paul? Hmm, I doubt it. It's more likely he's fouled me and is helping me up, or maybe he's calling me a lucky so-and-so for the equaliser I had just scored. Mind you, if my goal with my standing leg was jammy, so was his opener, which was deflected past Edwin van der Sar by Michael Carrick.

We gave an exceptional performance that night, and deserved to win by more than the 3–2 scoreline, but we weren't complaining about totting up three goals in Milan, where we'd come unstuck a few times in the past.

There was a time when it seemed Ronaldinho was joining United and we were all looking forward to it. But he chose Barcelona, perhaps thinking the lifestyle in Spain suited him better, possibly having heard some scurrilous rumours about the rain in Manchester! He would have fitted in well at United – he's a happy person, an entertainer who's always wearing a wide smile, much like Dwight Yorke, with no malice in him whatsoever.

◄ After all the joint history, all the growing up together, it seemed weird to be facing David Beckham in such a big match as AC Milan against Manchester United. But the game, as ever, takes precedence over personal feelings and you just have to get on with it. It must have been particularly difficult for David because he's always been such a massive fan of United, as well as a legendary player. Here he had tackled me and then picked me up, made sure I was all right. That's typical because as well as being a top-class footballer, he's also a top-class person.

When we get back together the years melt away and we're basically the same two lads who started our careers at United, even though we've followed our different paths. There is never any awkwardness between any of the half-dozen of us who came through at the same time. We've never drifted apart through distance; we'll always be friends because we have a special bond – and it's unbreakable.

❛ *Probably this was the only time I tackled Scholesy – and I said sorry as quickly as possible!* ❜

DAVID BECKHAM

◄ David looks considerably happier than me during the second leg at Old Trafford, even though we were 3–0 up when he came on for the last half-hour.

He would still be trying hard, like the brilliant professional he's always been, but he knew his team was about to go out of Europe and in this moment he was being his usual friendly self while enjoying the feeling of being on the United pitch again. As for me, I wasn't up for any banter because, despite our lead, which eventually stretched to four goals on the night, I was concentrating hard. Hence the Scholes scowl!

I would find it difficult to put myself in Becks' shoes on this occasion because I couldn't possibly imagine being in a big game at Old Trafford and playing for the opposition. I know it was hard for him, but although I saw him briefly after the game, he had to get away to the airport with his team so there was no chance to discuss how he felt.

When David left United he was somewhere near his peak and it was disappointing to lose such a top player, but you have to accept it in this game because people move on all the time. Ryan, Gary and me have been lucky exceptions to be at one club for so long.

I never felt I had said goodbye to United after so many great years there. Even though we lost, it was a special night to go back to United and play against my old mates. The crowd reaction was incredible.

DAVID BECKHAM

▲ This is the strike that took me past an immensely satisfying milestone, my 100th goal in the Premier League. It arrived at Wolverhampton in March 2010 and what made it even more welcome was that it was the only goal of a tense game. To be honest, it had been a long time coming since I had been made aware of the approaching century somewhere in the nervous nineties. I'd scored my ninety-ninth at West Ham three months earlier, and despite a few near-misses the ton was proving elusive.

When it came, after seventy-three minutes of a scrappy stalemate at Molineux, I must admit it was a tidy effort. I got the ball in the box, managed to sidestep a couple of lads and slammed it in the bottom corner.

The nice thing was that my son Arron was there with his grandad, my wife Claire's father. Being an absolute United fanatic with an amazing knowledge of the club – ask him about any game in the last three years and he'll give you every detail – Arron was well aware of the goal's significance. He's at senior school now so he's allowed to go to the away games that don't involve too much travelling – the likes of Blackpool, Wigan, Blackburn, Moscow . . . well, he couldn't be sent to bed early that night, could he?

➤ First on the scene to celebrate my century – and, more importantly, to acclaim the fact that United are ahead – is Michael Carrick, a real Rolls-Royce of a footballer who I love to have alongside me. He's terrific on the ball; he's a wonderful athlete with all the attributes demanded of a central midfielder, and he's very cultured, very relaxed in his style.

His passing stands out but he also contributes hugely to the team by quietly breaking up attacks, reading the game and making interceptions with those long legs. He's got a goal in him, too – the one up at Wigan as we were closing in on the title in 2009 comes to mind, as does his spectacular effort in the 7–1 win over Roma – yet still he can be described as an unassuming, unobtrusive performer.

It's fair to say, too, that Michael is the same on the field as he is off it. Essentially, he's a calm, modest lad who doesn't spend much time in the public eye. He's not always going out or doing interviews, and sometimes in such cases the recognition can be lacking. But even if he doesn't always get the appreciation he deserves from fans and the media, then certainly he is highly valued inside the club and in the wider game. He's another one who was given a new deal by United in 2011, and he is well worth it.

It's been the ultimate pleasure to play alongside Scholesy and to learn from him; how he looks after himself, how he trains, how he deals with certain situations in games, little things he does to find space. It's not that he set out to teach me, but he was as fine a footballer as I ever came across and so much just rubbed off. On a personal level we get on really well. He's a normal, down-to-earth lad whose family means everything to him, similar to myself in that he just gets on with life and enjoys his football. His sense of humour, though, is something else. He likes to throw in little one-liners here and there to stir the pot. He can cut someone down to size with one devastating comment, and when he tosses something in it tends to be the final say.

MICHAEL CARRICK

▼ You might say snarling and pointing my finger is no way to behave on a lovely sunny spring afternoon, but I just couldn't help myself towards the end of our visit to Blackburn in April 2010. The fellow who upset me was Vince Grella, Rovers' Australian midfielder, who I believed had gone down rather too easily when I made contact with him. Even so, I must admit to being surprised to see quite so much anger in my face in the photo, and I'd guess frustration was magnifying my feelings. We were chasing the title and needed to win, but we had missed a couple of chances and the game was moving inexorably towards a 0–0 draw, which wasn't good enough for us.

What am I saying? Certainly not inviting him out for a drink that evening! Meanwhile Ryan seems to be dissociating himself from my unseemly behaviour. 'That Scholesy, what's he like?'

◀ I'm getting to grips with Carlos Tevez in the Manchester derby at Eastlands in April 2010, a game which was destined for such a tumultuous finish. So many United fans were devastated when Carlos left because he was an exciting and talented player, and they loved the effort he put into every game. I think it's a shame he went, too, especially to City, and he's done fantastically well for them as we knew he would. But I could understand that he wasn't getting enough starts to satisfy him after Dimitar Berbatov arrived, and that prompted his decision.

Carlos was an infectiously lively person to have around the place. We changed next to each other, and got on famously, even though we did have a bit of history. When he was a teenager he played against us for Boca Juniors and after I tackled him he called me a butcher. Imagine, the cheek of that! But from the day he joined United we were fine together. We were both competitors and we had a few battles in training, but although there was a bit of a language barrier – we didn't go in for deep philosophical discussions – we respected each other for the football that we played. As a creative midfielder, I found him a dream to play with because of his constant movement and hunger for the ball. He was always available and each of us knew what the other one needed. Certainly, when Carlos Tevez departed, I missed him.

▲ For the sheer, undiluted joy of the moment, this injury-time winner against City on their own ground on a gloriously sunny Saturday lunchtime in April 2010 was the most satisfying goal I've ever scored.

I know there was the long-range effort against Barcelona which put us into the Champions League final two years earlier, but that was about pure achievement. This was altogether more personal for a United lad putting one over on City, who were beginning to spend vasts sums of money and starting to think they were becoming a big club.

That day we had played okay without being brilliant, but it looked as though we were going to drop two crucial points in the race for the championship. Then, at the last gasp, in came a cross from Patrice Evra on the left, and from somewhere

I'd dredged up enough strength that late in the game to get into the box. There wasn't much pace on Pat's delivery so I had to generate all my own power by leaning forward and throwing my head at the ball. In those circumstances I didn't attempt to place it, I just aimed to hit the target, and sure enough it bounced just inside Shay Given's post. For a Manchester United man, life couldn't get a lot better than that.

▼ I'm turning away to celebrate the triumph over City, while the cavorting Dimitar Berbatov looks reasonably pleased with life, too. I'm not too sure where he learned to dance like that, but I'm pretty certain it wasn't Salford!

◄ There was a price to pay for all that euphoria following my winner against City. Gary Neville grabbed me and gave me a lingering kiss which was all over the newspapers and the internet the next day. I must admit I did take a lot of stick for it, even from my own kids, but honestly I didn't mind. We were both that happy, and I think the picture just shows how passionately Gary feels about the game and what had just happened.

I won't say we both felt exactly the same because *he* came and kissed *me*, and I never had the slightest intention of giving him even a peck. Had I realised what he was going to do I might have made sure I was up at the other end of the pitch, or at least turned my cheek. But he didn't give me time. I just thought he was going to say well done or something equally moderate, then the next moment he's smacking his lips on me. Weird or what? But I didn't care – it was a complete spur-of-the-moment thing. I'm sure that it wasn't something that had built up inside him over time. At least, I hope it wasn't . . .

> *I'm an incredibly emotional person on a football pitch, and when United scored a last-minute winner against City, especially one which revived our hopes of the title, well, it felt like one of the greatest moments you could possibly imagine. We were all so happy; Paul's a great friend and I just gave him a kiss.*
>
> *It wasn't planned, I can assure you. We didn't even mention it to each other after the game. Nobody really saw it at the time, but one photographer picked it up and for three days it was all over the newspapers. I suppose I can understand why, because it looked so intimate – certainly it gives a whole new meaning to passion in football!*
>
> *Mind you, when I rang a friend on the way home, he told me: "I don't blame you. I'd have gone further than that, I was that happy." So you might say that Paul got off pretty lightly on the whole . . .*

GARY NEVILLE

16

NINETEEN – AND OUT

Towards the end of yet another tumultuous season in 2010/11, in which United won their nineteenth League title – beating Liverpool's long-held record in the process – but were forced to bow the knee by Pep Guardiola's magnificent Barcelona side in the Champions League final at Wembley, I made a momentous personal decision.

My body was making it amply plain to me that, at the age of thirty-six, it was time for me to retire. The manager was kind enough to tell me I could have carried on a bit longer, limiting my number of appearances, but that didn't feel right for me and so I called it a day.

Though I consider myself unbelievably lucky to have enjoyed such a long career packed with so many highlights, I can hardly believe that it is all behind me now. The time has absolutely flown by, and it seems like only yesterday that I was starting out as a slightly tubby little teenager with everything to prove.

◀ Chewing the fat with Edwin van der Sar, one of the greatest goalkeepers I've ever seen. He always had something to say and was very forthright at our team meetings, though here it looks like he's listening to me for a change. As a performer, Edwin seemed to get better with age, which was amazing because he was one of the few people still playing who was older than me.

When I used to face him in his Fulham days I never thought I was going to score because he was such a massive presence between the posts; he just filled the goal. And it wasn't just his work keeping the ball out, his kicking was fantastic, too. He comes from Holland, a footballing country in which everybody strives to be good on the ball. As a youngster at Ajax he would have been made to use his feet, and that stood him in good stead for the rest of his career.

There were campaigns to make him change his mind about retiring, but Edwin is a man of his word. He's so fit I'm sure he could go on playing until he was forty-four or forty-five, but he made his decision to leave after 2010/11 and everybody had to respect that.

❛ *I enjoyed a chat with Paul, we had a lot in common. He's a private individual and I recognise that in him because I'm also a little bit like that. Some people don't see the necessity of talking to the press all the time. You're here to do a job on the football pitch, that should be enough.*

Paul brought so much quality to his work, so much composure on the ball, so many goals when he was younger. When I was in Dutch and Italian football, a lot of people looked at Manchester United, and when they were asked who was the best player, a lot of them said Paul Scholes. Much of what he did looked simple, but actually it was quite hard. Invariably he controlled the ball instantly and passed it straight on, keeping the game moving. He made inch-perfect passes across the pitch; he saw the gaps and could play the ball through them. So it didn't surprise me that so many top-class international footballers recognised his quality.

For the future, I believe he can become a successful coach if he sets his mind to it. "Tell them, show them, coach them" is what you have to do, and Paul can show them anything. It's a great start. ❜

EDWIN VAN DER SAR

➤ When Ryan Giggs put away a difficult volley against Newcastle at Old Trafford on the opening day of our 2010/11 campaign, he extended his remarkable record of being the only man to score in every Premier League season, and I was delighted to help him on his way. It was late in the game, and we were 2–0 up when the ball came to me in a bit of space and I just knew – that old telepathy again – that Ryan would be running towards the left of Newcastle's box. I didn't have to look, I'd have been stunned if he hadn't been there, and as the ball dropped he put it away sweetly into the far corner. It was a special moment for Ryan, good for him to get the milestone out of the way in his first match, and I wouldn't be surprised if he keeps the sequence going for a few more seasons yet.

Joining us for the celebration is Dimitar Berbatov, who had scored earlier in the game and went on to a superbly prolific term, knocking in twenty-odd goals by the spring. Because of his naturally relaxed style, some people reckon he doesn't work as hard as he might, but I can assure them he does. He's quick and strong, too, but what he's really all about is producing the unexpected. There's just that little bit of the Cantona about him; he can do astonishing things with the ball. As a character? He's like most centre forwards – if he's scoring goals then he's happy.

❛ *Our combination for this goal summed up a lifetime in football together. Without even raising his head, Paul knew where I'd be, how I wanted the ball played, the precise weight of pass required. He knew I wasn't going to run in on goal, but that I'd hang back, knowing he'd find me. Perfect.* ❜

RYAN GIGGS

▲ This was the 150th time in my senior United career that I'd experienced the sheer ecstasy that comes with scoring a goal, but I can swear, hand on heart, that the glee on my face is down to putting United in front at Fulham rather than the reaching of that personal mark. I had Antonio Valencia and Dimitar Berbatov to thank for setting me up for a twenty-yarder which I caught quite nicely and it went into an unguarded corner.

Running up for a quick cuddle is Patrice Evra, who has been a revelation for United after an awkward little settling-in period, starting with a baptism of fire at City. He watched and learned, saw what was needed in the English game, and then emerged as one of the best fullbacks in the world. He's so small that a lot of people think he might be a soft touch, but he's very strong in the tackle, he can run all day, he's a brilliant overlapper and he's hardly ever injured.

Sad to say our visit to Craven Cottage didn't end too happily for us. We were 2–1 up near the end when Nani missed a penalty, then Brede Hangeland equalised at the death.

▼ 'Two minutes to go, ref?' That's the only construction I can put on this gesture, made during what ended up as a near-disastrous visit to Goodison Park in September 2010. During the first minute of stoppage time we were 3–1 up and apparently cruising, but by the final whistle the score stood at 3–3 and Everton had missed a decent chance to score what would have been a sensational winner.

It wasn't typical of us, it was more something we tended to do to other teams, and the only positive spin we could put on it was that it was early in the season so there was plenty of time to recover. The manager's reaction? Let's say it was interesting . . .

▲ Awareness of the ever-changing situation around you is absolutely essential to a central midfielder, so it's no good staring at the ball at your feet. Obviously you must have it under control, but your eyes have to be raised, looking for passing options all the time, as these two shots demonstrate. That's something I shall strive to pass on in my new career as a coach.

> *Paul always had fantastic technical ability – his awareness, touch, range of passing were remarkable. He played as though he had eyes in the back of his head. I had a video made of him to show the other boys how he looked both ways before receiving the ball – what we call the windscreen-wiper technique. He's the best I've ever seen at that by a million miles. Since then, wherever I have coached, I have told the players to watch Paul Scholes. No wonder Zinedine Zidane is among his admirers – and for someone of that stature to wax lyrical about Paul speaks volumes.*

BRIAN KIDD

▲ I never grow a full beard. This is about as far as it gets because after that my wife starts complaining and my kids moan that it hurts when I give them a kiss.

I'm remarkably cheerful here given that I'm occupying the bench, though as you get older you have to expect to spend more time as a substitute, and you realise that there's no point in being too grumpy about it.

◄ Let me admit straight away that this tackle on Pablo Zabaleta, for which I was sent off in the FA Cup semi-final against Manchester City at Wembley in April 2011, did not make for pretty viewing. I have watched it a few times on TV playback and it looks very nasty, not least because of the distinctly ferocious expression on my face in the instant before my studs make contact with the Argentinian defender's leg.

But, hand on heart, I didn't have the slightest intention of catching him like that. I'm not malicious and it was a complete accident. The ball bounced high between us and the only way I could go for it was by raising my boot. The same applied to Zabaleta and he was doing exactly the same thing. Where it went grievously wrong for me was in my timing. I was a fraction late, the ball had gone and there was no way I could stop my boot following through on to his thigh. As to the fierce look on my face, that's just down to putting everything into my effort to make the challenge. I was sorry the lad was hurt, but a moment's thought should tell anyone that it wasn't a deliberate assault. After all, why would I do that, knowing the inevitable consequence?

The referee had no alternative but to send me off, and I had no argument about his decision. It spoilt my weekend, and a lot of United supporters' weekends, too, which didn't make me feel good. It was hard to get over it, the incident preyed on my mind for a few days, but in the end you can only put it behind you.

It was a hugely frustrating experience for us because after missing a couple of chances in the first half we weren't playing as well as we should have been, and after we had gone behind we didn't really look like equalising. Then my tackle really put the kibosh on our chances.

One thing I must make clear, though. The red card had no bearing whatsoever on my subsequent decision to retire at the end of the season. The manager wondered if I'd let it influence me, and I put his mind at rest on that one. I've never been one to act on impulse, and this was no exception.

▼ So it's goodbye from me, but not from him! I think you can tell here that the tension has lifted after we clinched the championship with a nervy draw at Blackburn in our penultimate game, but while I was contemplating imminent retirement, Ryan had no such thoughts. He played superbly at Ewood Park, as he did all season, having really taken to life in central midfield. He's got everything needed for the role – his trickery from being a winger, he can find a pass, he can tackle, he's a great athlete. I always thought the position was made for him and he can play there until he's forty. And to think that the pundits had been expecting me to be replaced by a younger man . . .

◄ It was a weird situation. There I was walking out to face Blackpool behind skipper-for-the-day Edwin van der Sar, who was making his farewell home appearance before retirement, and the only people in that jam-packed stadium who knew it was also *my* last competitive match at Old Trafford were the manager, my wife and the kids.

How did I feel? A little bit ill, to be honest. There was a sick feeling in the pit of my stomach as I realised I would never make this walk again at the Theatre of Dreams with the same genuine job in front of me. Part of me felt I should have announced that I was packing it in so I could say goodbye at the Blackpool game, though I knew I could make my farewells to the fans at my testimonial a few months later and I felt that with the Champions League final just around the corner, it would be better all round if there were no distractions.

When I glanced over my shoulder, it was fantastic to see the number nineteen picked out in the crowd, signifying that we had broken Liverpool's record number of titles. It was a good game, too, against an entertaining Blackpool team, and although I was delighted to finish with a win, I was sorry to see them go down.

As for my retirement, I've only ever known one way of making my living, and I've only ever worked for one employer, so it might be considered a difficult decision to step aside after twenty years at Old Trafford, seventeen of them involved with the first team. In one sense, of course, it was. I love the club with a passion; the fans have treated me brilliantly right from the beginning; the way of life has suited me down to the ground, and the game has been amazingly good to me. I have never stopped counting my lucky stars that I have been able to forge a career, and a secure future for my family, out of doing something that is so much fun.

But when I examined my options in the spring of 2011, and if I was scrupulously honest with myself and everybody else, there was only one thing I could do. I knew in my heart that it was time for me to go. I was thirty-six years old and most of the time I was on the pitch I was no longer feeling great physically; my legs were going, I was slowing down. I'd played about thirty games in the season and I hadn't done too badly, but I didn't think I'd been contributing enough. I know there wasn't pressure for me to be scoring goals any more, but I couldn't shake the feeling that a central midfielder for Manchester United should be capable of hitting the target on a fairly regular basis. Not only that, I felt I wasn't setting up many goals, either.

The manager was great, telling me I could still play twenty-five or thirty games for at least another season. He didn't try to lean on me; he just wanted me to be certain I had made the right decision. The fact is that if I stayed on I'd want to be in the team when the big games came around, and I totally understood that, at my age, that wouldn't always be possible. For my money, if you're in the squad you should be able to start games and last the ninety minutes. Regrettably, I'd not done that for a while. In some games during 2010/11 I could barely break into a run and that just won't do. Could I have played on at a lower level? Well, if Oldham had wanted me, and if only I'd had the legs, then I'd have given it a go. But I knew in my heart that my days as a professional footballer were over.

So it's time to think about what to do next. I don't really know anything else but football, so I think that's got to be my working future and I'm gearing towards that at the time of writing by getting my coaching qualifications. I hope I've learned something over my twenty or so years at Old Trafford and that I'll be able to help young players to develop. The manager has mentioned a future for me coaching at United, and that is my plan. I only hope I can put something back into the game, which has treated me so handsomely for so long, and I'll be doing my utmost to justify the faith the club continues to show in me. I know there's hard work ahead, but my enthusiasm for the game burns as brightly as ever, and I can hardly wait to get started.

▲ I never tired of the communal celebration after the presentation of the Premier League trophy, which we finally got our hands on after beating Blackpool at Old Trafford on the last day of the season, although we'd sewn up the title a week earlier. The whole squad is in this shot and it gives me a chance to mention lads who haven't cropped up earlier in the book.

We had loads of stand-out performers in 2010/11, none more deserving of praise than Ji-Sung Park, here grinning towards the left of the middle row in front of the roaring Tomasz Kuszczak. Ji has made a fabulous contribution to United since his arrival in 2005. He doesn't stand out as a flashy performer, but he can do anything and is so underrated. He runs all day, he's got terrific touch, he's more aggressive on the pitch than many people realise and he's particularly effective when it comes to the big games. In South Korea he's loved, even worshipped – his locker at Carrington is always spilling over with his fan mail – and he's a very popular lad with the United players, too.

Quiet like Ji, and another fantastic professional who never complains about anything but just gets on with his job, is Antonio Valencia, wearing number twenty-five on the right. You won't find a better athlete in the game; he's a steely individual, highly motivated, and he's got exceptional quality. He's actually a right-winger but he's one of our best defenders, too, as he showed in the Champions League against Chelsea by dropping to right-back when Rafael was injured.

One of the more enthusiastic singers, next to the ever-exuberant Anderson on the right of the front row, is Javier Hernandez, an outgoing, happy lad who is always smiling and lighting up the place. For my money he's the buy of the 2010/11 season and he proves that if you put in the graft then you get the rewards. I've never seen a footballer work harder. At 9 a.m. he's always in the gym, putting in an hour's preparation for training, and afterwards he'll take another hour to warm down and do his weights. The result of his dedication, added to his amazing talent, can be seen on the pitch, where his movement is unbelievable. It makes life so much easier for his fellow attackers.

Smack-bang in the centre of the picture with the trophy at his feet is another young newcomer who has done remarkably well, the defender Chris Smalling. His purchase was a masterstroke by the manager – he must already be worth double what United paid for him – and he's going to be a top player. He's another lovely, unassuming fellow, yet more proof that invariably Sir Alex gets it right where character is concerned as much as in football terms.

A word, too, for the Da Silva twins, revelling with Wayne Rooney on the left – just don't ask me which is which because I never have a flipping clue! They both have fabulous ability; they made a big impact this time around and they are destined to become top players for United. They can get the hump in training when the tackles fly in, but they can hand it out, too, and basically they're a pair of happy Brazilian lads with a very bright future.

Another top-quality defender is Jonny Evans, crouching between Ji and Vida. He might look slender but he's immensely strong and very talented, rather reminiscent of the young Gary Pallister. His only problem will be getting past Rio and Vida, but he's got plenty of years ahead of him. The same challenge confronts another Irishman, the midfielder Darron Gibson, here sat directly behind Ando. He's got everything it takes to be a success in football, though he does need to make his breakthrough in 2011/12. I wish him, and the rest of the lads, all the luck in the world.

▼ Somebody actually took the trouble to add up the ages of Ryan, Edwin and myself – seen here holding each other up as we brandish the Premier League trophy in the Old Trafford dressing room – and they came up with the outlandish figure of 113. I must point out that I was the baby of the trio, and it might also be worth adding that you can't beat experience. After all, we had just won the title.

▼ A snap from happy hour at the old folks' home? It could hardly be that, with the feller on the left looking so sprightly and contemplating the next phase of his phenomenal career. As for the rest of us, the class of '92 relished the opportunity to be reunited in the Old Trafford dressing room for Gary Neville's testimonial match against Juventus a few days before our Champions League final date with Barcelona.

It was magical for Ryan, Nicky, David, Gary, Phil and me to be in each other's company again, and to play together for the first time in some eight years. Everything felt right, both on the pitch and off it. Footballing-wise, we just slotted back together seamlessly, knowing exactly what the other lads would be doing and what they required.

On a personal level, it was even better. After the game we sat around nattering for ages and were the last ones to leave. It was as though we'd never been apart and nobody wanted to go home. We should do it more often.

➤ How do you beat Barcelona? Ask me another . . .

If you said this summed up Manchester United's experience in the 2011 Champions League final, then I wouldn't be inclined to argue. From the puzzled expressions and the rather forlorn head-scratching of the manager and myself, you might conclude that the picture was taken after the game. Actually, it was during a training session at Wembley the day before, when we genuinely believed we could lift the trophy. Oh well, back to the drawing board . . .

◄ I spent the last few minutes of my professional career pitting my wits against this fantastic footballer, Lionel Messi, and his brilliant Barcelona teammates after being called from the bench near the end of the Champions League final at Wembley. By then, we were 3–1 down and the game was all but up, although you never know what might have happened if we had managed to pinch another goal.

I don't think I've played with or against a better player than Messi. He's right up there with the likes of Zidane, Figo, Rivaldo and Ronaldo, and will go down as one of the all-time greats. He's almost like a little lad in the playground at school, the way he twists and turns with the ball, keeping it when it seems impossible. And then there are his fifty goals in a season – truly remarkable!

➤ I've never been one for collecting shirts, but it meant a great deal when Andres Iniesta asked me for a swap at the final whistle and I was more than happy to agree. He's someone I've always admired and respected, without doubt one of the best players in the world, and it was a memorable moment.

That said, my expression makes it clear that, like young Fabio da Silva at my side, I'm not exactly feeling like the life and soul of the party as I watch the Barcelona players celebrate on the Wembley pitch.

◄ With my loser's medal around my neck, I can only applaud Barcelona after they beat us in the Champions League final at Wembley – and I have no hesitation in admitting, albeit through gritted teeth, that they were by far the better side once again. Just as in Rome two years earlier, we never really got to grips with them, managing only one shot on target, which tells its own story.

Their passing was mesmerising – out of this world. You get the feeling that you could play six or seven against them in midfield and they would still dominate the possession. You know exactly how they're going to play but you can't stop them. They have their own philosophy: the Barcelona way. They always stick to it, they don't change it for anybody, and you can only admire them for that.

Of course, it was disappointing to end my career on a losing note, but we have to remember we'd come up against one of the greatest teams there has ever been. They have set a standard for Manchester United to aspire to – that is the goal now – and I see no reason why it cannot be attained over the next few years. I know the manager won't stop trying to lift United to that exalted level because he can never resist a challenge – and, take it from me, he's a long, long way from the finishing line.

➤ My time as a professional footballer ended on a fantastic note when New York Cosmos – complete with director of soccer Eric Cantona and club president Pele – rocked up at Old Trafford for my testimonial match against Manchester United in August 2011.

It was a fabulous night and I couldn't have imagined it working out any better. There was a full house at my home ground where I had played since I was nineteen years old, I scored a goal and we won 6–0 – perfect! My only worry was making the speech after the game, but I got through that somehow and then I was able to relax.

My relationship with the fans has always been brilliant – they do take to a Manchester lad – and they gave me a send-off I'll never forget. I hope I have left them with a few decent memories.

Lining up with me for the pre-match presentations are David Gill, Eric, Sir Alex and Pele. I could not have wished to bow out in more illustrious company.

◄ It was an amazing experience to walk around the ground at the end of the game with my family, waving an emotional farewell to the fans. Earlier Claire had sworn she wouldn't join us on the pitch, but she did and that capped the whole night for me. Normally I don't relish the spotlight, but this was the best possible way to finish as a Manchester United player.

I was delighted, too, that a percentage of the proceeds from the testimonial will be used to help children with autism, a cause very close to my heart.

17

HOME IS WHERE
THE HEART IS

The God-given ability to make a football do more or less what I want it to – though not always, obviously! – has given me a standard of living that I could never have dreamed of had I left school to take up any other job accessible to me. What might that have been? I haven't got the faintest idea because it never entered my head that I would ever be anything else but a footballer. That said, I didn't even dwell on a future in the game. The truth is that I didn't agonise over anything as a kid; I just got on with life and, incredibly fortunately for me, it led me to Manchester United.

But for all the benefits that professional football has brought me, none of them would mean a thing to me without my family, my wife Claire, my sons Arron and Aiden, and my daughter Alicia. We are happy where we live – on the edge of Saddleworth Moor to the north-east of Manchester. I'd like to echo the words used by Sir Bobby Charlton in a recent television documentary about his remarkable life. He said, 'I've been a lucky, lucky lad.' And that says it all for me, too.

▲ My new generation of Red Devils, three kids who keep Claire and me extremely busy, but we wouldn't have it any other way. I know I'm bound to say this about my own children, but we think they're brilliant and we love them to bits. The oldest is Arron, who is now twelve; his sister Alicia is ten and little Aiden is six.

▼ Lifejackets all round for Claire, Alicia and Arron on a boat trip to see the dolphins near our house in Portugal, which is our favourite holiday location and where we go every year. We didn't take Aiden on this jaunt – he was busy playing with his grandparents on the beach.

Claire and I met in a pub in Middleton when we were about eighteen, which means we've been together for half our lives. We got married in 1999; she's given me three terrific kids and we couldn't be happier.

She's never been hugely into football, which has suited me fine. Sometimes I could come home from a match and she wouldn't even know who we'd been playing. There would be no agonising over what had happened on the pitch, which helped me to wind down and to relax away from my work. That was so important, especially as I could be in a rotten mood for a couple of days if I'd had a bad game, although having the kids has been ideal for taking me out of myself and reminding me what really matters in life. It's not that Claire didn't care about my football. She went to most home games and didn't miss the really big occasions, but it was never a passion with her.

She's a tremendous mother, always coping marvellously when I've been away so much with United and England, though we've been lucky in that her mum and dad live nearby and are always ready to help out. That's put my mind at rest, too, when I've been on my travels, knowing that Claire has got someone she can rely on.

▲ Arron in action for his team, Stalybridge Celtic, for whom he scores a goal or two. He loves other sports, too, especially cricket, but he's been into football since he was tiny. He's a massive Manchester United fan, it's a passion inside him, and I'm sure it'll last all his life.

Arron's got a fantastic memory and can tell you everything about any of United's games over the last few seasons. Even though I've retired now, we'll be going to every home match, and doubtless quite a few of the away ones, too. But there's more to the lad than sport – he seems to be clever at school and gets good marks in all his subjects.

◄ Alicia is another natural at sport, very quick around the netball court and willing to have a go at practically anything. She's also massively into riding. She's got a nice little pony called Boston; they do all the local shows together and they've won a few rosettes.

My daughter is not quite as mad on United as my eldest son, but then, that would be difficult! Still, she enjoys coming to the games and I think she liked keeping an eye on her dad.

▼ Aiden suffers from autism and has quite severe learning difficulties, so he can't take part in most sports at the moment, though he does absolutely love his swimming. He seems in his element in the pool; he's a real water baby and it's wonderful that he's got that to enjoy. Some children with autism are scared of water, but Aiden's the opposite. He'd be swimming every minute of the day if he could, and on holiday we even feed him in the pool.

We hope his condition improves, but we're not banking on it, just doing everything we can to make sure he has a happy life. He has a load of people trying to help him, speech and play therapists for example — anyone who might be able to improve his ability to communicate. Aiden's in his own little world, and it is some consolation that he does seem content in it. We always do all we can to involve him in everything we do, but we never force him into anything that he's not comfortable with.

▲ Aiden's not always in the mood for this sort of picture, but this shot was perfect. He loves being tickled and the other two know how to get him to enjoy himself, then to keep still for the camera. To me, this just shows how much they all love each other, and there's nothing better than when your kids get on like that.

Arron and Alicia are fantastic with Aiden. It can't be easy having a brother in his situation, but they cope with it brilliantly. They don't always get much attention from him, which is all a part of autism, but they still put the effort in and they still show him love. And he loves them in return, you can tell that.

▲ This is one of my favourite pictures, with the Scholes family all looking so smart – even me for a change! It was our tenth wedding anniversary in 2009, when we had a ceremony to renew our vows and then a tremendous do in the evening to celebrate our decade of married life. You see, really I'm just an old romantic at heart . . .

◄ We've always been a close family. On the left are Claire's mum and dad, Phill and Marie, and on the right are my parents, Marie (what a coincidence) and Stewart.

▲ You might recognise a few faces here as four of my oldest mates in football join in the craic on the night of the tenth anniversary bash. I seem to be spinning a line to Nicky Butt, which is amusing Phil Neville rather more than his brother Gary, while Ryan Giggs has eyes only for the camera. It looks like a beer or three has been consumed and I'm sure there were a few more in the offing. We've had plenty of good nights together over the years, and this was no exception.

▲ Claire and I relaxing at a wedding do — somebody else's this time.

▲ The kids were delighted to meet their dad's double when we visited Disneyland in 2010. It was boiling hot in Florida, the queues were horrendous and I don't know how I survived, but Arron, Alicia and Aiden had a fabulous time, which is all that mattered.

As I hope anyone who reads this book will realise, my family means the world to me. However sad I might be to retire from playing football – and it comes to us all sooner or later – knowing I have the support of Claire and the kids in whatever I do is a wonderful feeling. Then there is my second family, Manchester United, which I won't be giving up. After all, I'll still be going to work at Carrington every day, so I'm not complaining. Life goes on – here's to the next chapter.

A WORD FROM
SIR BOBBY CHARLTON

Let me start by making a little confession. In my position as a director of Manchester United, I know I shouldn't have favourites, but I'm only human and I must admit it – Paul Scholes *is* my favourite.

In fact, I'd go so far as to say that, for a long time now, he has been my footballing hero. I don't think anyone will mind, or have their feelings hurt, if I own up to that because the lad is an absolute diamond, both as a player and as a person.

Most of my time these days is spent watching the games from up in the stands. When you're on the board you get the good seats so you can see everything, the whole picture, and in game after game, even in the last months leading up to his retirement, that confirmed my opinion that Paul was a master, a sensational performer, one of the finest in the world.

You saw how he found space by moving away from his markers before they realised what was in his mind. Then, having engineered the room in a crowded midfield, he passed the ball like a dream, long or short, whatever was demanded.

There are some players who have a lot of talent but they can only see what's happening right under their noses. But Paul had unbelievable peripheral vision, seemingly taking in the whole of the pitch. Suddenly, out of nothing, he would ping a superb pass and you would hear people sitting near you, men who knew the game, gasping in wonder. 'How did he do that?' they'd ask. 'He didn't even look!' They knew they were in the presence of something special.

Another thing I loved about Paul is that he demanded the ball all the time, he wanted to influence the game, to win the game. A lot of people will attempt to hide in the shadows if it's a hard battle but he was the opposite, always available, anticipating the next move, taking responsibility, and he was like that every time he ran on to the field.

Then you come to his goals. He always scored them by the bucketful, lots of them absolute crackers from outside the box, and also there were plenty with his head, even though he's a little 'un. He had that precious instinct for popping up at crucial times, such as right at the end of the Manchester derby at Eastlands in the spring of 2010, when he nodded the winner with virtually the last touch of the match.

He was brave, too, hard as nails and never afraid to put his foot in. In fact, if there was one fault in Paul's game it's that when he was cut, he bled, and occasionally he wanted revenge. When that happened – and really it was not very often – he was oblivious to what people were shouting at him, he just couldn't help himself, but that was part of him and you couldn't change it. Denis Law had a bit of that, too, and what a player he was.

Even though he's in his middle thirties and contemplating a future as a coach, I still think of Paul as the same little lad who played for United's youth team in the early 1990s. I recall asking the coaches if there was a chance of any good kids coming through to senior level, and they astonished me by saying there were five or six definites. Next I asked who was the pick of the bunch, and nearly all of them said Paul Scholes.

When I saw him in action I knew exactly what they meant. He was so young and tiny, but his quality was exceptional. He had guile, an amazing touch and that priceless knack of making instant decisions that catch so many opponents on the hop.

In short, he always possessed that indefinable, special ingredient that goes into the making of a star. Yet through all the years, with all the magnificent success he has enjoyed, he has remained the same lovely, unassuming individual he was when he came to the club.

I always pop into the dressing room after a match to have a word with the players. With Paul it tended to be 'well played' because invariably he had. He'd just give me that little grin of his and he was always so modest and down to earth, no matter how brilliantly he might have performed out on the pitch.

I believe he's happy with his world. He's got his family, he's proud of being a Manchester lad, he's delighted to be with the club he's always wanted to play for, and now perhaps serve in another capacity. I couldn't picture him being anywhere else. Paul Scholes is just magic and we have been so lucky to have him. It's no wonder he's my favourite!

MY CAREER IN FIGURES

Manchester United 1994/95 to 2010/11

HONOURS

Champions League: 2007/08
Premier League Championship:
1995/96, 1996/97, 1998/99,
1999/2000, 2000/01, 2002/03,
2006/07, 2007/08, 2008/09, 2010/11
FA Cup: 1995/96, 1998/99, 2003/04
League Cup: 2008/09

*Substitute appearances in
brackets. 'Others' includes FA
Charity/Community Shield, UEFA
Super Cup, FIFA Inter-Continental
Cup, FIFA Club World Cup.*

1994/95

League: 6 (11) games, 5 goals
FA Cup: 1 (2) game, 0 goals
League Cup: 3 games, 2 goals
Europe: 0 (2) games, 0 goals
Total: 10 (15) games, 7 goals

1995/96

League: 16 (10) games, 10 goals
FA Cup: 0 (2) games, 1 goal
League Cup: 1 game, 2 goals
Europe: 1 (1) game, 1 goal
Total: 18 (13) games, 14 goals

1996/97

League: 16 (8) games, 3 goals
FA Cup: 2 games, 2 goals
League Cup: 2 games, 1 goal
Europe: 0 (4) games, 0 goals
Others: 1 game, 0 goals
Total: 21 (12) games, 6 goals

1997/98

League: 28 (3) games, 8 goals
FA Cup: 2 games, 0 goals
League Cup: 0 (1) game, 0 goals
Europe: 6 (1) games, 2 goals
Others: 1 game, 0 goals
Total: 37 (5) games, 10 goals

1998/99

League: 24 (7) games, 6 goals
FA Cup: 3 (3) games, 1 goal
League Cup: 0 (1) game, 0 goals
Europe: 10 (2) games, 4 goals
Others: 1 game, 0 goals
Total: 38 (13) games, 11 goals

1999/2000

League: 27 (4) games, 9 goals
Europe: 11 games, 3 goals
Others: 3 games, 0 goals
Total: 41 (4) games, 12 goals

2000/01

League: 28 (4) games, 6 goals
Europe: 12 games, 6 goals
Others: 1 game, 0 goals
Total: 41 (4) games, 12 goals

2001/02

League: 30 (5) games, 8 goals
FA Cup: 2 games, 0 goals
Europe: 13 games, 1 goal
Others: 1 game, 0 goals
Total: 46 (5) games, 9 goals

2002/03

League: 31 (2) games, 14 goals
FA Cup: 2 (1) game, 1 goal
League Cup: 4 (2) games, 3 goals
Europe: 9 (1) games, 2 goals
Total: 46 (6) games, 20 goals

2003/04

League: 24 (4) games, 9 goals
FA Cup: 6 games, 4 goals
Europe: 5 games, 1 goal
Others: 1 game, 0 goals
Total: 36 (4) games, 14 goals

2004/05

League: 29 (4) games, 9 goals
FA Cup: 5 (1) games, 3 goals
League Cup: 1 (1) game, 0 goals
Europe: 7 games, 0 goals
Others: 1 game, 0 goals
Total: 43 (6) games, 12 goals

2005/06

League: 18 (2) games, 2 goals
Europe: 7 games, 1 goal
Total: 25 (2) games, 3 goals

2006/07

League: 29 (1) games, 6 goals
FA Cup: 3 (1) games, 0 goals
Europe: 10 (1) games, 1 goal
Total: 42 (3) games, 7 goals

2007/08

League: 22 (2) games, 1 goal
FA Cup: 1 (2) game, 0 goals
Europe: 7 games, 1 goal
Total: 30 (4) games, 2 goals

2008/09

League: 14 (7) games, 2 goals
FA Cup: 1 (1) game, 1 goal
League Cup: 2 (1) games, 0 goals
Europe: 3 (3) games, 0 goals
Others: 3 games, 0 goals
Total: 23 (12) games, 3 goals

2009/10

League: 24 (4) games, 3 goals
League Cup: 1 (1) game, 1 goal
Europe: 7 games, 3 goals
Others: 0 (1) game, 0 goals
Total: 32 (6) games, 7 goals

2010/11

League: 16 (6) games, 1 goal
FA Cup: 2 (1) game, 0 goals
Europe: 4 (3) games, 0 goals
Others: 1 game, 0 goals
Total: 23 (10) games, 1 goal

OVERALL

League: 382 (84) games, 102 goals
FA Cup: 30 (14) games, 13 goals
League Cup: 14 (7) games, 9 goals
Europe: 112 (18) games, 26 goals
Others: 14 (1) games, 0 goals
Total: 552 (124) games, 150 goals

Only three men have exceeded
Paul Scholes' total of 676 senior
appearances for Manchester United.
They are Ryan Giggs (876, with power
to add), Bobby Charlton (758) and
Bill Foulkes (688). In fifth place is
Gary Neville (602).

England 1997 to 2004

66 full caps: 64 starts, 2 subs, 14 goals

ACKNOWLEDGEMENTS

Claire, Arron, Alicia and Aiden;

Claire's mother and father, Phill and Marie, for always being there for the family when I've been away from home;

My mother and father, Stewart and Marie;

My Uncle Pat, for giving me such great support over the years;

Sir Alex Ferguson for everything, including his generous foreword;

Sir Bobby Charlton for his lasting inspiration, and his warm afterword;

Harry Swales for his kindness and assured guidance;

Ryan Giggs for all his help with this book.

Finally, for only talking about the good bits: David Beckham, Steve Bruce, Nicky Butt, Michael Carrick, Sven-Goran Eriksson, Rio Ferdinand, Darren Fletcher, Paul Gascoigne, Glenn Hoddle, Kevin Keegan, Brian Kidd, Wilf McGuinness, Albert Morgan, Gary Neville, Phil Neville, John O'Shea, Gary Pallister, Wayne Rooney, Teddy Sheringham, Ruud van Nistelrooy, Edwin van der Sar.

Paul's collaborator, Ivan Ponting, would like to thank:

Pat, Rosie and Joe Ponting;

Rhea Halford for her refined editing and publishing skills;

Kerr MacRae, Rory Scarfe and Leigh Ann Broadbent of Simon and Schuster;

Proofreader Lorraine Jerram and designer Jacqui Caulton;

Cliff Butler, Manchester United's mastermind;

John Peters of Manchester United and Getty Images, Andy Cowie of Colorsport, Hayley Newman at Getty Images, Lucie Gregory at the Press Association, David Scripps at Mirrorpix, Billy Robertson at Action Images, Mark Leech at Offside, Patrick Mooney;

Karen Shotbolt of Manchester United;

Jack Rollin; David Wilson; David Welch; Les Gold.

PICTURE CREDITS

Action Images

vi, 16 (above and below), 17, 19 (below), 24, 36, 38 (above), 39 (above), 43, 47, 49, 50, 53, 57, 67, 68, 73, 75, 78 (left and right), 95, 103, 114, 126, 127, 128, 144, 147, 153, 155 (below), 178, 189, 192, 199, 202, 209, 212, 222, 244, 247, 246, 252, 254, 255, 257, 258, 259, 261, 264, 280 (below)

Colorsport

11 (above), 13, 14 (below), 19 (above), 22, 23, 29, 32, 33, 44, 52, 54, 56, 59, 60, 62, 63, 64, 66, 76, 79, 81, 82, 83, 84, 90, 93, 99, 100 (above and below), 108, 111, 113, 118 (right), 119, 134, 136, 161, 172, 176, 217 (below), 232, 241, 269, 271, 272

Getty

3, 25, 26, 27, 30, 45, 46, 55, 61, 69, 70, 71, 72, 77, 86, 88, 97 (above), 101, 109, 112, 115, 116 (above and below), 118 (left), 122, 125, 129, 133, 135, 138, 139, 140, 142, 143 (below), 145, 149, 150, 154, 155 (above), 156, 162, 163, 165, 170, 171, 174, 175, 184, 185, 187, 188, 190, 191, 193,194, 195, 196, 200, 201 (above and below), 204, 205, 206, 208, 210, 211, 213, 214, 219, 224, 225, 228, 229, 230 (above and below), 234, 235, 237, 238, 239, 243, 245, 247, 248, 250, 262, 273, 276, 278, 279, 280 (above), 281 (above and below), 282 (above and below), 294

Mirrorpix

9, 10, 20, 40, 51, 98 (above), 169, 179, 223, 226

Offside

11 (below), 12 (above), 12, (below), 14 (above), 18, 28, 34, 35, 37, 38 (below), 39 (below), 48 (left), 85, 87, 89, 92, 96, 97 (below), 98 (below), 102 (above and below), 104, 105, 106, 107, 117, 123, 124, 130, 132, 143 (above), 146, 148, 160, 164, 182, 203, 216, 221, 231, 236, 260, 267, 275

Press Association

42, 48 (right), 94, 110, 152, 166, 167, 168, 173, 177, 180, 181, 197, 198, 215, 217 (above), 218, 220, 227, 240, 242, 251, 253, 256, 263, 266, 268, 270 (above and below)

Topfoto

58, 120, 131, 141

Courtesy of Manchester United

74

Courtesy of Paul Scholes

6, 7, 8, 284, 285, 286, 287, 288, 289, 290, 291, 292, 293